CW01457284

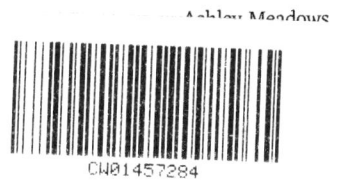

Bonsai for Beginners

Learn 10 Speedy Steps in 14 Days or Less to Take Care and Make a Healthy, Evergreen Tree. Easy Mastery for the Time-Strapped

Ashley Meadows

© Copyright 2024 by Ashley Meadows
All rights reserved

The content contained within this book may not be reproduced, duplicated, or transmitted without direct written permission from the author or the publisher. Under no circumstances will any blame or legal responsibility be held against the publisher, or author, for any damages, reparation, or monetary loss due to the information contained within this book, either directly or indirectly.

Legal Notice:

This book is copyright-protected. It is only for personal use. You cannot amend, distribute, sell, use, quote, or paraphrase any part, or the content within this book, without the consent of the author or publisher.

Disclaimer Notice:

Please note the information contained within this document is for educational and entertainment purposes only. All effort has been executed to present accurate, up-to-date, reliable, and complete information. No warranties of any kind are declared or implied. Readers acknowledge that the author is not engaged in the rendering of legal, financial, medical, or professional advice. The content within this book has been derived from various sources.

Please consult a licensed professional before attempting any techniques outlined in this book. By reading this document, the reader agrees that under no circumstances is the author responsible for any losses, direct or indirect, that are incurred as a result of the use of the information contained within this document, including, but not limited to, errors, omissions, or inaccuracies.

Table of Contens

Get Free Bonus: "Organic Gardening Book"

"Get All The Support And Guidance You Need To Be A Success At Organic Gardening!"

This Book Is One Of The Most Valuable Resources In The World When It Comes To Starting Your Own Organic Garden Fast And Easy!

Scan QR and Get this Book For Free

Preface

Welcome to the world of Bonsai, where the majesty of the forest is packaged within the confines of a single pot. When you hold this book, consider it a doorway into the ancient art of growing miniature trees. It is a craft that reflects the majesty of nature but requires nothing more than patience, creativity, and knowledge, and you will find them in this book.

I am pleased to present Bonsai for Beginners, a guide designed for beginners. If you are admiring the beauty of these little trees and asking yourself, "How do I begin?" You are in the right place at the right time. On the pages of this book, you will find answers to your questions.

In this book, you will find a guide to action and an understanding of what Bonsai is. You will learn that it is both a science and an art. A meeting place of disciplined care and artistic expression. Your Bonsai journey will become a mirror of life itself in many ways. It will teach you to care and beauty.

For those who have long admired these miniature plants, rest assured that the art of Bonsai is more accessible than it may seem. I've put together this guide to break down the basic elements of Bonsai growing into easy-to-understand, practical advice. Chapters on history, selection, shaping, planting, and care will help you confidently grow your first Bonsai.

It's wonderful that you are holding this book in your hands. Let the pages inside guide and inspire you. As your first Bonsai grows and takes shape, you will find joy and satisfaction. Numerous Bonsai lovers have already found them whispering in the leaves of these living sculptures.

Get ready to get your hands dirty, look at your Bonsai with pride, and indulge in your favorite hobby. Welcome to the beginner's path to Bonsai mastery. The journey begins now.

Introduction

B y opening this book, you enter a new chapter of your life. Your life will be filled with peace, discipline, and joy. This book is designed as a comprehensive journey that will allow you to learn the art of Bonsai and grow your first tree.

The quiet art of Bonsai has flourished for centuries in the serene corners of gardens. This book is a tribute to this art, your ticket to the world of Bonsai. After reading this guide, you can create your own Bonsai tree. I will be your guide on every page of the book.

Have you noticed the charm these small trees create? They are the zen of minimalist beauty and the pride of their creators. Bonsai is like a snapshot of nature's greatness, transformed by your hands into a harmonious miniature statue.

This book is written to remove the cloud of doubt that often shrouds Bonsai growing. Here, you will find clear instructions and simple tips that will give courage to even the most timid beginner. You will learn how to choose suitable trees, understand the importance of watering and soil quality, and master the basics of pruning and shaping a tree.

You will also become familiar with the principles behind Bonsai - the styles and forms that have been refined over time to express grace and beauty. Your tree can turn into a small forest, and every year it will grow and delight you.

Each page in this reading brings you one step closer to understanding. You will encounter terminology that may have once puzzled you, but here, the explanation is simple and concrete.

Practical recommendations will turn the manual into a narrative about ancient art. The practice of Bonsai continues to grow, evolving with every artist who picks up the scissors.

You will revere Bonsai and develop a similar respect for this unique form of tree growing. After all, the most profound lessons resonate with our intuition and creativity. I hope you will learn the mechanics of Bonsai and feel its spirit. You can join an ancient tradition and a community of modern enthusiasts.

We are going on this journey together. You bring curiosity, and I bring knowledge. It will help you join this creativity. Let's start introducing the elegance of Bonsai into your life. Welcome to Bonsai for Beginners.

CHAPTER 1

About Bonsai

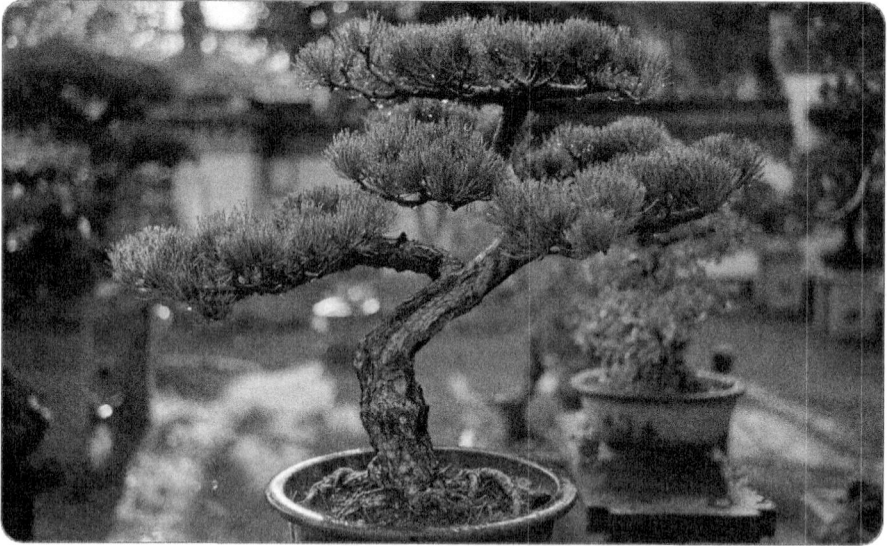

Picture 1: Japanese white pine (Pinus parviflora).

F or many people, Bonsai brings to mind images of Asia and ideas about esoteric practice, which takes a lot of time to master. Bonsai has now become an international art form. This is an accessible hobby for everyone, no matter where they live. It is a complex combination of artistry and horticultural skill, allowing people to create living masterpieces. These small trees can outlive their creators, which excites the mind.

It is generally accepted that Bonsai originated in ancient China, with evidence of plants being grown in containers dating back to Babylonian times. However, it is important to clarify an important distinction: not every potted plant can be called a Bonsai. Before delving into the history of Bonsai, it is crucial to understand what Bonsai is in a modern context.

Welcome to the Art of Bonsai

Bonsai is an art. It's about growing tiny trees that have the spirit of big ones. When you make a Bonsai, you create a little piece of nature in your home. You shape it. You care for it. To start, pick a tree. Think about where it will live — indoors or out? Each spot has a different kind of tree that likes it best. Then, find a pot. It should be the right size for your tree. Not too big, not too small.

Next, you'll learn to trim. Cutting the branches makes your tree look just right. You choose how it looks. Tall, short, or like it's out in the wild.

Water and soil are essential, too. Not too much, not too little. Just like Goldilocks' porridge, it needs to be just right.

With time, your tree grows. You watch. You adjust. That's the art. It's slow but fun—you and your tree are making art together. Let's start your journey to the art of Bonsai.

Simple Bonsai Basics

Have you ever looked at a Bonsai and said, "I want to try that!" Well, you are in the right place. Making Bonsai is a lot of fun and easier than you think. Let's get down to some basic stuff. First, understand that a Bonsai is not a tree. What we do to a tree makes it a Bonsai. You can create one of many types of trees or shrubs. The key is to choose a plant that you like, suitable for where you will be growing it: indoors or outdoors.

Pots are the part of your composition. Bonsai means "plant in a pot" in Japanese. The pot holds the roots and serves as a stage for your tree. Pots come in different shapes, sizes, and colors. Choose one that matches your tree and its position.

Part of the Bonsai look is that the tree seems old. This is called "tree character." You build it over time by trimming and shaping the tree. Anything from scissors to wire could be your tools. Techniques for trimming and shaping are essential to learn.

Keeping your Bonsai healthy is a must. That means knowing about water, food, and light needs. Every tree is unique.

How does Bonsai work?

Let's start learning Bonsai basics and how to turn an ordinary tree into a miniature miracle. We'll use the proper techniques and steps to ensure you create something unique.

Bonsai works on the principle of balance. You have a tree and a pot, and you have to maintain stability. The roots should not be too crowded; otherwise, they will suffocate. But they must also remain strong enough to hold the tree firmly in the pot and collect water and nutrients well.

Imagine a tree in the wild. It grows towards the sun, fights the wind, and takes root deep into the ground. When we create Bonsai, we imitate these conditions. We want our tree to look like it has seen the sun, the wind, and many years while still being small enough to live in a pot.

To get there, we start with pruning — cutting back branches and leaves. This lets us shape the tree and encourage growth where we want it. But pruning isn't just about cutting; it's about planning. Where should the branches go? How can we make the tree look balanced?

Then there's wiring. This is like braces for trees. We use wire to gently direct branches to bend and twist naturally. It takes careful hands and time, as branches need to be shaped without harm.

Now, let's talk about the roots. Root pruning happens every couple of years. By trimming the roots, we keep the tree small and stop it from outgrowing its pot. This might sound scary, but it's a big part of keeping your Bonsai healthy.

Watering is next. Too much water and the roots rot. Too little, and the tree dries out. It's about giving your Bonsai just enough. The way to water changes with the seasons, the tree type, and even where the tree lives.

Nutrition is crucial, too. Trees need food to create those beautiful leaves and strong branches. With Bonsai, we use special fertilizer to meet the needs of our mini trees without going overboard.

And we can't forget the sunlight. Like all plants, Bonsai trees use light to make food and grow. Each tree has its own sweet spot in sunlight. Some love a sunny window; others need a bit of shade.

Lastly, we adjust for the seasons. Just because a Bonsai lives with you doesn't mean it's forgotten nature's calendar. It still needs to rest in winter, bloom in spring, grow in summer, and prepare in fall.

This is the life of a Bonsai, a cycle of care and growth. It's a partnership between you and your tree. You learn from it, and it grows from you. That's how Bonsai works — a bit of nature's wisdom in your home.

Why is Bonsai so popular?

So, what is so special about Bonsai? Why do people around the world love these small trees so much?

Let's start with history and culture. Bonsai has deep roots dating back to China's distant past. It carries stories and traditions that are part history, part legend. This cultural gem is key to understanding the art of nature.

Then there's the hobby side. Bonsai gives you a break from the hustle and bustle. It's a slow hobby in a fast world. After a long day, caring for your Bonsai can feel like hitting the pause button. Caring for it is easy - watering, pruning, just observing. It's about being in the moment and that's something special these days.

But Bonsai is a difficult hobby! People love a challenge, and Bonsai offers that. There are many things you need to think about, such as how the plants work and what they like. Plus, there's also an art to making your tree look the way you envision it. And this is possible thanks to careful care. You can't rush Bonsai because it grows at its own pace and teaches patience and attention to detail.

Artistry is another magnet. Bonsai allows you to become an artist without using paint or canvas or a sculptor without a hammer or clay. Your tools are just scissors and wire. Your canvas is now alive and green. Every Bonsai tree is your sculpture, and you sculpt it every day. It's very personal and cool to express yourself through living sculpture.

Now, let's look at the community. Bonsai brings people together. Clubs, forums, a whole community that shares tips, stories, and even seeds.

For many, it is friends and a shared passion that illuminate the Bonsai experience. Improving your well-being has other benefits. Bonsai can beautify a place and make it look alive and fresh. People enjoy seeing greenery indoors, and caring for a living thing has its benefits. It is said that a hobby like Bonsai can help you cope with stress and anxiety and even improve your ability to concentrate.

Let's not forget about the environmental aspect. In our concrete-filled world, Bonsai is a way to reclaim a piece of nature. It reminds us that even with limited space, we can care for the environment. This is a big plus for many who live in places where gardens are a luxury.

And these tiny trees tell tales. Every Bonsai has its own backstory - how it was grown, shaped, and even saved can make people become attached to their trees. People become attached to and value their Bonsai over the years, watching them mature and change.

There is something universal about Bonsai, too. It doesn't matter where you come from or what language you speak. Bonsai is a bridge between cultures, an art form everyone can appreciate. This versatility is a powerful attraction.

At its core, Bonsai is a mixture of art and science, hobby and craft, culture and society. It is a rich and rewarding practice, loved by people, young and old, everywhere.

CHAPTER 2

A short history of Bonsai Art

Picture 2: Chinese juniper (Juniperus chinensis).

B onsai experts like myself ponder this question daily. During my apprenticeship, while toiling late into the night, this same question arose repeatedly. It's a highly subjective and personal matter: some view Bonsai as an ancient Asian art form, while others see it as an intricate form of gardening. Some perceive it as a spiritual journey, while for others, it's simply a hobby. In truth, it encompasses all these perspectives and more.

When I was asked to define a Bonsai, the shortest and most profound answer I could get was: "It's a small tree in a pot." However, within this simple statement lies depth and richness - a fusion of art and horticulture, incorporating elements of design, culture, spirituality, craftsmanship, and discipline.

Understanding the essence of Bonsai begins with the word itself. In Japanese, "Bonsai" is made up of two characters: "bon", which means tray or container, and "sai", which means "planting". Thus, any potted plant can technically be called a Bonsai. However, there is a massive difference between a young houseplant in a plastic pot and a centuries-old pine tree blooming in an antique Chinese container.

The crucial difference between a potted plant and a true Bonsai lies in the intentional influence of human hands. Bonsai is carefully created, shaped, and grown to imitate the essence of nature. This goes beyond simple gardening because it requires a focused creative process. And this process is sure to be filled with artistic sensitivity and sophistication.

From an aesthetic point of view, the appeal of a Bonsai lies in the grace and dignity of a centuries-old pine or other plant that has flourished throughout its life in a pot. To appreciate a Bonsai requires a level of involvement that goes beyond the superficial appeal of bright flowers or lush foliage found in conventional potted plants.

In any human endeavor, especially in art, there is an inherent element of artificiality. This paradox is especially evident in Bonsai: excessive ego can ruin the natural beauty of a design, but leaving everything to nature can result in a dull appearance. The appeal of Bonsai lies in striking a delicate balance between human intervention and natural growth.

From a Western perspective, Bonsai defies categorization—it is neither pure art nor horticulture, neither craft nor science. Using Bonsai requires a holistic approach that combines artistic vision with technical skill to create beauty and significance. Without attention to aesthetics, technical skills remain ineffective; without the ability to promote healthy growth, creative expression is weakened. Bonsai is a living testament to this subtle symbiosis. This dynamic art form evolves not only with the passage of time and seasons but also through the creative contributions of successive owners.

A Bonsai tree that has survived centuries represents a deep history, testifying to the care and nurturing of countless people. Its gnarled bark, gnarled branches, and unique character tell stories of resilience and adaptation. Bonsai transcends individual ownership and fleeting moments—it is a timeless art form with a legacy that extends far into the future.

How did Bonsai evolve?

Bonsai is an art form based on ancient traditions. It started over a thousand years ago in China, where people made tiny landscape paintings on trays called Penjing. This art features small trees and nature scenes. Later, the idea migrated to Japan. The Japanese focused more on trees and made them look like natural giants. Over time, they created the art of Bonsai that we know today.

Bonsai means "planted in a container" in Japanese. These mini trees aren't a special kind of tree. They're regular trees but grown in a unique way to stay small. In Japan, people used Bonsai to decorate and for peace of mind. Bonsai became very famous. It was a hobby for everyone, not just the rich.

Then, Bonsai spread to other places, like Europe and America. Now, people all over enjoy growing these tiny trees. Bonsai shows and clubs popped up, sharing skills and tree stories.

Today, Bonsai is a mix of art and gardening. It's loved by many for its beauty and the patience it teaches. Each little tree tells a story, living through years under the care of its owner.

Main stages of formation and evolving

Let's trace the timeline and explore the key stages in the development and formation of this art form.

The ancient roots

You already know that the journey of this Art began in ancient China more than a thousand years ago. We discussed the early manifestation of Bonsai art, known as 'Penjing'— miniaturized landscapes, complete with tiny trees, rocks, and even water features. Here marks Phase One, a stage of ingenuity and philosophical reflection, where the goal was to capture the essence of nature's grandeur in a compact form. Chinese monks and scholars used Penjing to tell stories of harmony between humans and the cosmos, setting the stage for an art form that would traverse cultures.

The Japanese version of Bonsai Art

Moving to Phase Two, Bonsai art finds a new home in Japan. Likened by how a playwright adapts a story to a new audience, Japanese enthusiasts refined and tailored the art to their vision and environment. The focus shifted from the landscapes of Penjing to the individual tree, plucking a single character from a broader cast to shine in solitude. This period is marked by dedication to minimalism and the nuance of single elements, shaping what is now recognized as Bonsai.

The meticulous shaping of these trees reflected the disciplined approach to life characteristic of Japanese culture. The essence of Japanese Bonsai art is the pursuit of simplicity and elegance. His goal is to create an image of the great dramas of nature within the confines of a pot—a wrinkled pine tree resisting harsh winds or a cherry tree blissful in its bloom.

Symbolism plays a vital role in the Japanese Bonsai tradition. Favorites include trees such as pines, junipers, and maples, each representing qualities such as hardiness, purity, and peace. Trees become living haiku, poems in their short form that have an impact far more significant than their physical size.

Adapting to the times

Through the peaceful Kamakura and Muromachi periods in Japan's history, Bonsai saw a broadened appreciation and diversification of styles. This marks Phase Three—the stage of growth and variation, where Bonsai began to be exchanged as gifts of honor and showcased in collections. It transitioned from the preserve of the elite to a pastime of the wider populace.

The Edo Period: A 'Golden Age'

The flourishing Edo period heralded Phase Four, akin to a 'golden age' in Bonsai history. Bonsai artistry reached new heights of creativity and refinement, with attention to every detail, from pot selection to cultivation techniques. During this era, Bonsai truly stepped into the limelight, with government sanction and support extending its influence.

Bonsai on the World Stage

Transitioning to Phase Five, Bonsai began its global odyssey. After Japan opened its ports in the mid-19th century, Bonsai was showcased to international visitors, marking its move onto the world stage. As it spread to the West, enthusiasts began to interpret Bonsai through a different lens, integrating local plants and contemporary designs. This stage was a fusion, blending Eastern tradition with Western innovation.

Bonsai in Present Days

Today's Phase Six sees Bonsai as a mature global art form. Modern Bonsai artists have more information and tools than ever, and their work continues to innovate without losing connection to its roots.

There's a sense of stewardship among the Bonsai community to preserve tradition and encourage personal expression. Technology now allows for broader dissemination of knowledge, with online communities and international exhibitions, making the Bonsai stage more inclusive and vibrant.

Technology plays a significant role in Bonsai's present-day story. Online communities buzz with activity as people worldwide share their success stories, swap tips, and offer support. Learning has been democratized; with a few clicks, a beginner can watch detailed tutorials, order tools and trees, or participate in webinars, making the art more accessible than ever.

Innovation in tools and cultivating methods has also evolved. From sophisticated watering systems to LED grow lights for indoor trees, the paraphernalia available to Bonsai enthusiasts now marries tradition with the cutting edge. The art is evolving as practitioners experiment with non-traditional species and styles, adapting to different climates and personal tastes.

The modern Bonsai market is also a window into its popularity. Specialty nurseries selling Bonsai and pre-Bonsai (young trees meant for Bonsai training) are more common, and the trade in Bonsai-related paraphernalia is booming. Similarly, Bonsai classes are in demand, not only in person but also online, reflecting a genuine desire for mastery of the form that transcends geographical boundaries.

Throughout history, Bonsai is a fusion of philosophy and horticultural skill. Each stage of its development added depth, creating a picture of living art that spoke the language of nature.

You are now just as likely to find a Bonsai on your office desk as in a traditional Japanese garden. It has become a hobby for everyone - city dwellers with limited space, retirees looking for a quiet time, and even busy professionals looking for peace. The charm of forming and caring for a Bonsai tree transcends age and culture, proving its universal appeal. Despite changes in practice and perspective, the essence of Bonsai remains constant: to evoke the full grandeur of nature within the constraints of an artfully crafted miniature.

Bonsai testifies to mankind's eternal desire to create and cultivate living nature. As Bonsai continues to grow in homes and gardens worldwide, each tree is a testament to the scope and sustainability of this ancient art.

Each Bonsai nurtured today continues a narrative, 600 words rich and thousands of years deep, sprouting from ancient traditions to a future still taking root.

CHAPTER 3

Ten the most popular styles of Bonsai

C reating Bonsai is an expressive art form where trees are grown and shaped into specific styles to reflect various natural tree forms. Here, we delve into 21 styles admired and refined over centuries.

1. Formal Upright (Chokkan): This style mimics a tree growing in an open space with ample light. The trunk is straight and tapers cleanly from base to apex. It's the most classic Bonsai form, illustrating balance and stability.

Picture 3: Chinese juniper (Juniperus chinensis). Chokkan style.

2. Informal Upright (Moyogi): In this style, the trunk has slight curves but still generally points upward. It portrays a more relaxed image of a tree that has grown with a bit of wind influence.

Picture 4: Cotoneaster Bonsai tree. Moyogi style.

3. Slanting (Shakan): The slanting style represents a tree that has grown at an angle, often due to consistent wind or light direction. The trunk leans to one side, yet the tree remains balanced and elegant.

Picture 5: Chinese juniper (Juniperus chinensis). Shakan style.

4. Cascade (Kengai): Inspired by trees that grow over the sides of cliffs, the cascade style sees the tree top falling below the pot's base. It defies gravity and is dramatic in appearance.

Picture 6: Chinese juniper (Juniperus chinensis). Kengai style.

5. Semi-Cascade (Han-Kengai): The semi-cascade is less extreme than the full cascade. The tip of the tree bends down to the side and may reach just at or slightly below the pot's rim.

Picture 7: Japanese white pine (Pinus parviflora). Han-Kengai style.

6. Double Trunk (Sokan) and Triple Trunk (Sankan): This style boasts two or tree trunks growing from a single root system. One trunk is smaller, and the other is more dominant, creating a sense of depth and relationship.

Picture 8: Brush cherry Bonsai tree. Sankan style.

7. Split Trunk (Sabamiki): The split trunk style shows a tree with a trunk that appears damaged or hollowed out, similar to damage from natural causes, giving the appearance of age and survival.

Picture 9: Japanese white pine (Pinus parviflora). Sabamiki style.

8. Multitrunk (Ikadabuki): In multitrunk Bonsai, multiple trees emerge from one root system, resembling a small forest. The trunks vary in size and height, creating a natural woodland scene.

Picture 10: Korean hornbeam (Carpinus turczaninowii). Ikadabuki style.

9. Coiled Trunk (Nejikan): This style in bonsai, is a unique and captivating form that represents a tree with a twisted or spiraled trunk. This style is particularly striking and can evoke a sense of movement and dynamism in the bonsai composition.

Picture 11: Chinese juniper (Juniperus chinensis). Nejikan style.

10. Broom (Hokidachi): This style is characterized by a straight trunk with fine branching out at the top, similar to the shape of a broom. It's often used for deciduous trees with fine branching patterns.

Picture 12: Rockspray (Cotoneaster sp.). Hokidachi style.

There are many more styles of Bonsai, I try to make you understand that there are many of them. I hope you noticed that some styles are very similar, sometimes a combination of several styles. Therefore, it is sometimes difficult to attribute a plant to a certain style.

Each style tells a different story, evoking emotions and images of nature's resilience and beauty. From tempest-scoured coastal cliffs to serene forests, these styles offer a creative way to connect with the natural world through the art of Bonsai.

What is the difference between Bonsai styles?

Diving into the world of Bonsai, you'll find there's a forest's worth of different styles, each with its own unique twist. But what separates one style from another? Why choose a cascade over a formal upright? It's all about the story you want your tree to tell and the natural scenarios each style emulates.

The formal upright, or chokkan, stands tall and straight, like a tree that's grown unchallenged in an open space with plenty of sunlight. This style is all about strength and dignity, the image of the tree we often hold in our minds.

Then you have the informal upright, or moyogi, which is like the chokkan's more relaxed cousin, sporting a trunk with graceful curves. This style gives the tree a look that says it has weathered a challenge or two—like a gentle breeze shaping it over time.

Slanting, or Shakan, is the tree with a bit of a lean. It's growing towards the light or away from the wind and has a dynamic, dramatic touch to it. Cascade and semi-cascade styles depict trees that have faced off with gravity – the former plunging downward like a waterfall and the latter only slightly less so. Both mirror trees that dwell on cliffs or over water where they reach down towards the reflections below.

The literati, or bunjin-gi, is the poetic side of Bonsai. With its sparse foliage and often contorted trunk, it evokes an image of a tree battling for life on a rocky mountain, reaching upward from a sparse environment.

Take a step in another direction, and you meet the windswept look or fukinagashi. All the branches jut out as if blown by a strong wind. It's a style bursting with motion and tells of a life spent bracing against coastal gales.

The double trunk style, sokan, is where one tree has two trunks. It creates a mini-landscape in your pot, with one trunk typically smaller and younger than its partner. It's about harmony and contrast, the dance between two different growth stories from the same roots.

Some styles, like the multi-trunk and group plantings (ikadabuki and yose-ue, respectively), venture into creating forests in miniature. These styles aren't satisfied with telling just one tree's story – they want a whole cast of characters.

And not all Bonsai styles are defined purely by the direction of growth. The rock planting style, ishizuke, for example, has trees that have adapted to growing among the rocks, their roots gripping the stone. It's about tenacity and making the most of a hard place.

Every style has its own unique character. It's a different aspect of the relationship between trees and their environment. The variety in Bonsai styles allows you to capture the essence of other environments and moods – from tranquil forests to lonely mountain tops.

Choosing a style isn't just about the tree; you'll have to decide where you think the tree should go. What will it be - a windswept sea cliff or a complex mountain slope? This is where the whole difference between styles lies. Each style represents a different piece of nature's grandeur and lets you bring a landscaped corner into your home.

CHAPTER 4

Start your journey

T raveling through Bonsai is like sailing on a vast green ocean. It's a little scary but very useful. As you take your first steps into the Bonsai world, consider this chapter your compass, guiding you from curiosity to the land of tiny trees.

Preparation for beginning, decisionmaking

Starting your Bonsai journey is thrilling, but before diving in, some decisions need to be made. These choices will form the basis of your hobby and can affect the health of your Bonsai and the joy you get from the art. Let's explore the critical decisions that will shape your Bonsai adventure.

Here are tips and recommendations to help you make informed decisions that suit your lifestyle and interests.

Decision 1: Indoor or Outdoor?

Where will your Bonsai live? Will it grace your living room, or will it bask in the natural cycles of the outdoors? Your living situation and climate are big factors here. Indoor Bonsai can be trickier, requiring specific light and humidity. Outdoor trees can be more forgiving and naturally sync with the seasons.

TIP: Consider your living space and climate. If you have a garden or a balcony, outdoor Bonsai offer a wide range of hardy options and a more natural growth pattern. For example, Junipers and Pines thrive outdoors. If you're limited to an indoor space, look for tropical species like Ficus or Jade that can prosper inside.

RECOMMENDATION: Assess the amount of sunlight your space receives. An indoor Bonsai will need plenty of light, so a south-facing window is ideal.

Decision 2: Selecting a species

Which tree should you begin with? Various species have different needs and aesthetics. Some are more robust and better suited for beginners, while others can be demanding. Research the care requirements of potential trees and choose one that aligns with your climate and care ability.

TIP: Start with a forgiving species. Beginner-friendly trees are more resilient to fluctuations in care, giving you room to learn.

RECOMMENDATION: Research Bonsai species known for being robust and suitable for your climate. If unsure, a nursery specialist can recommend a species based on your environment. Below in this book, you will find the TOP 5 Bonsai recommended for a beginner

Decision 3: To train or not to train

Are you up for training a young tree, or would you prefer a pre-styled Bonsai that you maintain and refine? Training a Bonsai from scratch is a longer, more involved process but deeply rewarding. A pre-styled tree can offer instant gratification and a starting point to learn the ropes.

TIP: Consider a pre-styled Bonsai if you're new to the art. This allows you to learn maintenance techniques without the pressure of styling your own.

RECOMMENDATION: Once comfortable, you can progress to training a young tree, which will give you a fuller understanding of Bonsai cultivation. Below, we will look at this issue in more detail.

Decision 4: Defining your setup

Preparing your environment is vital. For indoor Bonsai, you'll need proper lighting, whether natural or artificial. For outdoor trees, consider protection from harsh weather. Also, decide on the style of pot and the type of soil, as each species has its preferences.

TIP: Invest in a good-quality pot and the right soil mix for your Bonsai. Proper drainage is crucial, so ensure your pot has holes and is of appropriate size for your tree.

RECOMMENDATION: Purchase or prepare a soil mixture that caters to your specific tree type, promoting healthy root development and moisture retention.

Decision 5: Time and commitment

Bonsai is a commitment. Do you have the time to water, prune, and care for these living sculptures? Understanding the time and attention your chosen species will need is critical. Set realistic expectations for what you can provide.

TIP: Realistically assess the time you can dedicate to your Bonsai. Different species can require varying levels of attention.

RECOMMENDATION: Choose a low-maintenance species if your time is limited, ensuring your Bonsai doesn't become a source of stress.

Decision 6: Learning the essentials

How will you learn about Bonsai care? Books, local classes, online forums, and clubs can all be excellent resources. Decide how you prefer to learn and seek out the best resources available.

TIP: Take advantage of beginner courses or local workshops. Learning the fundamentals from experts can accelerate your understanding and reduce early mistakes.

RECOMMENDATION: Gather essential tools like pruning scissors, wire cutters, and Bonsai wire before your tree arrives.

It's great that you are already reading these lines. However, here, we have compiled information for beginners to help you get started. You already understand that the world of Bonsai is much broader. And I know for sure you will need more information. But that will come later; now we have more important things to do.

Decision 7: Financial investment

Consider your budget for this new hobby. Costs can include the tree, tools, pots, soil, and possibly classes. Bonsai doesn't have to break the bank, but it's wise to anticipate expenses to avoid surprises down the line.

TIP: Determine a budget for your new hobby to avoid overspending. Start with the essentials, and you can always add to your toolkit later.

RECOMMENDATION: Compare prices and reviews for supplies and consider buying in bundles to save costs.

I hope you understand that the cost of these books is not the entire cost of your exciting new hobby.

Decision 8: Patience level

Are you patient? Bonsai's growth and development take time. You're in for a treat if you love seeing slow and steady progress. If not, you might need to cultivate patience along with your tree.

TIP: Accept that Bonsai is a slow art from the beginning. Progress can be measured in seasons, not days.

RECOMMENDATION: View each phase of your Bonsai's growth as an opportunity to practice mindfulness and appreciate the small changes.

We will touch on this aspect in more detail later in the pages of the books.

Decision 9: Joining the community

Will you go it alone or join the larger Bonsai community? Engaging with fellow enthusiasts can enrich your experience by providing support, inspiration, and camaraderie.

TIP: Bonsai enthusiasts often enjoy exchanging knowledge. Connect with a community to gain support and insights.

RECOMMENDATION: Join local clubs or online forums where you can ask questions, share experiences, and find encouragement.

Decision 10: Goal setting

What do you want from Bonsai? Is it relaxation, an artistic outlet, or a deep dive into horticulture? Your goals will guide how you approach learning and caring for your Bonsai.

TIP: Define what you want to achieve with Bonsai. Whether it's crafting a living masterpiece or simply enjoying a relaxing pastime, your goals will guide your approach.

RECOMMENDATION: Write down your Bonsai aspirations and revisit them regularly to stay motivated and on track.

Before you begin, take the time to consider each of these points carefully. Your decisions will lay the foundation for a fulfilling journey into Bonsai. With thoughtful preparation, your path will be clearer, allowing you to focus on the wonderful process of nurturing these captivating miniature trees.

Below, you will find chapters in which I tried to make your choice easier and make your immersion in the fantastic world of Bonsai as enjoyable as possible.

CHAPTER 5

Key decisions to make

I n this chapter, we will examine the key decisions that need to be made in detail. This will help you clearly understand what kind of Bonsai you need. As a result, you and I will avoid stupid mistakes, disappointment, and failure. Conscious choice brings us closer to success.

Step 1: Indoor or outdoor?

Choosing between growing Bonsai indoors or outdoors can affect your experience as a beginner. Any option has its advantages and disadvantages. Below, you will find some tips. They will help you make this critical decision.

Assess your environment

Start by observing the space where your Bonsai will live. Do you have a garden, terrace or balcony? The outdoor environment provides a wider range of tree species that can grow naturally. But if you live in an apartment and do not have outdoor space, then a Bonsai adapted for such conditions is more acceptable.

Consider the climate

Think about the climate you live in. If you experience cold winters, some trees may not survive outdoors without protection. In contrast, if you live in a mild climate, an outdoor Bonsai can benefit from the natural seasons, which are essential for many traditional Bonsai species.

Light and temperature requirements

Light is crucial for Bonsai health. Indoor trees need a lot of light, usually more than what's available indoors. If you choose an indoor Bonsai, you might need to supplement natural light with grow lamps. Outdoor Bonsais enjoy the benefit of natural sunlight, which is hard to replicate indoors.

Temperature is also important. Growing Bonsai indoors may require a stable temperature, away from drafts, heaters or air conditioners. All this can dry out your tree. Outdoor Bonsai are more tolerant of temperature fluctuations, but extreme heat or cold can still be harmful.

Watering and humidity

Watering needs vary greatly between indoor and outdoor trees. Outdoor Bonsai can often make do with natural rainfall, whereas indoor trees will rely on you for their water needs. Indoor air, especially in heated or air-conditioned homes, can be dry and may require additional humidity through misting or humidity trays.

Protecting from the elements

If you opt for an outdoor Bonsai, you'll need to learn how to protect it from harsh weather, like deep freezes or scorching sun. Understanding proper sheltering techniques, like using cold frames or shade cloths, can help your Bonsai survive and thrive.

Practicality and pleasure

If you enjoy spending time outdoors and have a garden, caring for your Bonsai outdoors can be more enjoyable. If you prefer the comfort of home and love greenery indoors, then you should choose an indoor Bonsai.

Please consider these suggestions carefully based on your environment, lifestyle and preferences. Choose the option that suits not only your circumstances, but also your level of commitment and interests. Remember that the decision you make will determine your Bonsai journey, so take the time to make wise choices.

Step 2: Select beginner-friendly tree

Choosing the right type of Bonsai is vital for a beginner. This can mean the difference between a frustrating experience and a rewarding experience. Here are a few thoughts to help you through the process of choosing the type that suits you best.

Once again, you will have to evaluate the choices you made earlier. Further steps and decisions greatly depend on it. Your local climate is the most critical factor. If you choose an outdoor Bonsai, then think about the climate conditions. Some species can tolerate a wide range of conditions, while others have specific needs. For example, if you live in an area with cold winters, look for species known to be hardy, such as pine trees or spruce trees.

Consider the lighting conditions and space available in your home or garden. Will your tree be exposed to direct sunlight, partial shade, or primarily indirect light? Be sure to choose a species that can do well in the lighting conditions you have to offer.

Consider how much time you are willing to invest. Certain species require more meticulous pruning and care, while others require less maintenance. Junipers, for instance, are hardy and can be a good choice for those with little spare time.

As a beginner, it's best to choose a species known for being robust and tolerant. The Ficus, Chinese Elm, and Jade (Crassula) are often recommended for novices because they are forgiving to watering errors and adaptable to a range of indoor conditions.

A species with a faster growth rate, like the Elm, can offer quicker gratification as it develops and changes visibly over seasons. Slow growers like Pines allow for more contemplation and can be less demanding but require more patience.

Understand the growth habits of different species. Some species might naturally grow large leaves or needles, which can be challenging to scale down to miniature proportions suitable for Bonsai. Deciduous trees will lose their leaves in the fall, which is natural but can be disconcerting to new enthusiasts if unexpected.

Don't hesitate to ask for advice from local Bonsai nurseries or clubs. People with experience in your particular climate will offer valuable insights into what species do well in your area.

Visiting a nursery allows you to interact with different species before choosing. You can observe the trees in person, touch them, and understand their texture and resilience.

Choose a tree that appeals to you visually and emotionally. The aesthetics, leaf shapes, bark textures, and overall forms vary widely, so pick a species that you find beautiful and resonates with you.

Approaching the selection process thoughtfully and considering these points will result in a more successful Bonsai experience. No matter which species you choose, remember that Bonsai is a journey, and starting with a tree that suits your environment and lifestyle will make the road much smoother.

I RECOMMEND STARTING WITH AN INDOOR BONSAI to make your first Bonsai experience as successful as possible. This will save you from painful choices and the need to consider many additional factors. However, your choice must be conscious. You can choose an external Bonsai and succeed too. But you must also be mentally prepared for the grief of defeat. Believe me, this path is not strewn with emeralds. This is work and patience, and the joy of success only becomes tastier.

Step 3: By or grow own tree from the seed?

For beginners, the decision to buy a preexisting Bonsai or start one from seed is significant. Each choice offers a different journey into the Bonsai world. Here are some suggestions to help you choose the path that's right for you.

Consider the time investment

Growing a Bonsai from seed is a lengthy process—it can take years before your sapling even starts to resemble one. However, if you relish the thought of nurturing a tree from its very origins and have the patience for long-term gratification, seeds could be a rewarding path.

On the other hand, buying a Bonsai means enjoying its beauty immediately. You'll also have a more assured outcome regarding the tree's health and shape. Buying may be preferable for beginners who are eager to learn styling and care techniques right away.

Think about your experience level

For those new to gardening, starting from seed may be daunting. It involves understanding germination, seedling care, and initial shaping. A pre-bought Bonsai allows you to focus on maintenance and learning care practices without the uncertainty of the seedling stage.

Reflect on the learning process

Growing from seed can be incredibly educational. You'll gain firsthand knowledge of a tree's life cycle and the factors that affect its growth. If the educational aspect excites you, this could tip the scales toward seeding. But, if you buy a Bonsai, especially one from a reputable seller, you can often receive care instructions specific to that species and plant. This guidance can be very beneficial as you're learning the ropes.

Analyze the costs

Growing from seed is generally less expensive initially, but remember that pots, soil, and fertilizers still represent an ongoing cost. Purchased Bonsai, especially more mature or exotic species, can be significantly more expensive but have the advantage of being already established and shaped.

Appreciate the options in styling

When buying a Bonsai, you may be limited to the pre-styled forms available at nurseries or shops. Growing from seed or sapling allows you the full creative freedom to train and style your Bonsai precisely as you envision it.

Enjoyment and attachment

Lastly, think about the emotional aspect. Some find a deep pride in seeing their Bonsai's entire journey from seed to tree. From this perspective, growing from seed can be a highly personal and satisfying experience.

FAQ:

> *Why is it beneficial for beginners to start with an older Bonsai tree rather than a young seedling?*

Starting with an older Bonsai tree offers several benefits for beginners. Firstly, older Bonsai trees already have an established shape and character, allowing new hobbyists to appreciate and learn from their existing structure. These mature trees are typically more resilient and forgiving, meaning they can better withstand occasional care mistakes that often occur during the learning process. They also require less time to achieve a finished appearance, providing immediate aesthetic enjoyment and a sense of accomplishment.

Additionally, working with older trees can provide invaluable hands-on experience in maintenance practices—such as pruning and wiring—without the long wait associated with growing a seedling. This helps beginners better understand the art and horticulture of Bonsai from the outset.

If you decide to buy, choose a tree that speaks to you—you'll spend a lot of time together. Look for a tree that's healthy, has an appealing shape, and suits your environment.

Whether you buy or grow your Bonsai, both routes are fulfilling.

Consider your goals, time, and resources to find the right choice for your Bonsai experience. Remember, the journey is yours—embrace it with enthusiasm and patience.

I strongly recommend not trying to grow your tree from seed. Of course, you can choose this path, but from experience, it is a mistake for a beginner. In almost all cases, you will fail. Over time, you will master this option to grow Bonsai. This book is for beginners, and my main goal is to inspire you with your success and excellent first experience. Therefore, your choice is clear: you are buying an unpretentious, ready-made Bonsai tree.

Step 4: Preparing your environment

Creating the right environment for your Bonsai tree is key to giving it a happy and healthy life. If you're on the fence about how to set up your Bonsai's home, here are some pointers that may help.

Assess the space

First, look around your place. Where do you spend most of your time? You might want to enjoy your Bonsai there. Make sure it's a spot where the tree can get its basics: enough light, good airflow, and a stable temperature.

Light is key

Find out how much light your Bonsai will need. Some trees crave lots of sunshine, while others like them more mellow. For indoor spaces, south-facing windows are great for light, but don't let leaves touch cold glass in winter. No sunny spot? You might need a setup with grow lights to keep your Bonsai cheerful.

Maintaining humidity

Our homes can be dry for indoor Bonsai, especially with heating or AC running. Bonsai trees like some moisture in the air. Placing a humidity tray beneath your pot helps. You can also mist your tree's leaves now and then. But don't go overboard – soggy and wet ain't good.

Think about temperatures

Bonsai trees don't like big temperature swings, so keep them away from drafty spots and heaters. If you're setting up outdoors, consider a spot that gets shade during the hottest part of the day to protect your tree from scorching.

Watering wisdom

Every species has its water likes. Many Bonsai trees prefer to dry out a bit between watering. When it does come time to water, it should be thorough. Think about easy access to water when you choose your Bonsai's spot. If your pot has drainage holes, what will catch the excess water?

Picking the pot

The pot is your Bonsai's home. Make sure it's the right size – not too big, not too small. It should have drainage holes to prevent water from pooling at the bottom. A good quality Bonsai pot can add to the overall beauty of your tree too. We'll discuss this topic a little later.

Soil considerations

Use the right soil mix for your type of Bonsai. It needs to drain well but still hold onto moisture. There's no one-size-fits-all with Bonsai soil, so you'll need to determine the mix best for your specific tree type and environment.

Protection from elements

For outdoor Bonsai, you must consider protection from harsh weather. Set a plan for when it gets hot, cold, or windy. Some types of Bonsai must be brought indoors during winter; ensure you have space for them if needed.

Accessibility

Position your Bonsai so it's easy to reach for regular care and admiration, but not in a high-traffic spot where it could get bumped or knocked over. Remember, your Bonsai is a living thing, not just decor. Treat it right by preparing an environment that'll help it flourish. As a result of your care and dedication, you'll enjoy watching your bonsai grow and thrive.

I recommend you choose your Bonsai tree's location as consciously as possible and consider the key factors described above. The most important things are stable humidity, temperature, sunlight, and accessibility. Your Bonsai should catch your eye as often as possible and bring you joy. Where exactly you place it is up to you.

Step 5: Time and Commitment

Investing in a Bonsai means you're investing your money, time, and commitment. It's vital to gauge whether Bonsai care fits into your lifestyle. Here are some insights to help you determine if you're ready to embark on the Bonsai journey.

Understand the responsibilities

Bonsai trees require consistent care, which includes watering, pruning, feeding, and inspecting for pests and diseases. Consider if you're ready and able to integrate these tasks into your daily routines.

Scheduling care

Think about your daily and weekly schedule. Can you set aside time for Bonsai maintenance? Unlike pets, Bonsai trees can be left alone for a day or two, but they still need regular attention. If your schedule is unpredictable, consider a species known for low maintenance, such as the Ficus.

Vacation planning

What happens to your Bonsai when you travel? Think ahead about who could take care of it while you're away. Preparing for these situations ensures your Bonsai continues receiving care even when you're not around.

Seasons change

Be ready for changes in care as seasons change. Your Bonsai will need different things throughout the year, like less water in the winter or protection from the hot summer sun. Read how each season affects your Bonsai to prepare for these changes. For indoor Bonsai trees this factor is minimal. However, it still needs to be taken into account. You can have a heater in the winter and an air conditioner in the summer. This is important for your Bonsai tree and you need to consider it at the site selection stage. The ideal place is away from air conditioners and heaters.

Learning and mastering skills

Are you prepared to learn new skills? As a Bonsai owner, you must understand techniques like pruning, wiring, and repotting. These skills take time to learn and even longer to master, requiring patience and commitment.

Regular observation

Good Bonsai care requires frequent observation to catch issues early—like brown leaves or dry soil—and address them quickly. This preventive care can avoid more significant problems down the line.

Honing your patience

Bonsai is not a fast hobby. Are you prepared to wait years to see significant growth or changes in your tree? It's almost meditative in how it teaches patience and appreciation for slow progress.

Budgeting time and money

Sure, there's a financial commitment, but there's also a time budget to consider. Whether it's regular care or the time spent at Bonsai workshops, ensure you're ready for this investment.

Emotional investment

Lastly, there's an emotional side to Bonsai care. These little trees can become dear companions, and watching them prosper (or sometimes struggle) can be an emotional experience. Investing your heart into the well-being of your Bonsai is part of the process.

These aspects of Bonsai care will help you decide whether you're ready for this commitment. If Bonsai seems right for you, it can be one of the most engaging and fulfilling hobbies, bringing calmness, a sense of achievement, and a connection to nature into your life.

Now, let's move on to organizational decisions. They may seem simple, and this is understandable. But this book should have this information. They need to be made. Don't you want to find out amid your hobby that you have no budget or no one to ask, or worse, your nerves are on edge, and you're nervous? No, you must understand everything from the beginning! And then an indescribable feeling of satisfaction awaits you!

CHAPTER 6

Organizational decisions to make

Step 6: Learning the Essentials

A solid understanding of the essentials is crucial before embarking on your bonsai journey. Here's how to ensure you have the foundational knowledge to start on the right foot.

Do your research

Begin with diving into the world of Bonsai through books, websites, and videos focused on Bonsai care. Familiarize yourself with the basics: watering, pruning, repotting, and the signs of a healthy versus an unhealthy tree.

Start with a single tree

When learning, it's tempting to buy several trees. However, starting with one allows you to focus on learning that particular species' care requirements and nuances without feeling overwhelmed.

Choose the right species for learning

Select a Bonsai species known for being beginner-friendly. Some species are more tolerant of irregular watering or slight variations in light and temperature, making them great for those new to the hobby.

Consider a starter kit

Bonsai starter kits can be beneficial for beginners. These kits often come with a young tree, proper soil mix, pots, tools, and sometimes a care guide. It's a convenient way to obtain all the essentials in one package.

Take a class or workshop

Look for beginner workshops or classes in your area. Hands-on instruction from an experienced teacher can provide invaluable insights you can't get from reading alone.

Join a community

Whether it's a local club or an online forum, surrounding yourself with fellow Bonsai enthusiasts can offer a support system. More experienced members can share advice and provide solutions based on their experiences.

Practice patience and observation

Learning to observe and be patient are essential skills in Bonsai. Pay attention to your tree's responses to care—you'll learn a lot by noting how it grows and changes with the seasons.

Learn the art of pruning

Pruning is both an art and a science. Learn the proper techniques to maintain the shape and health of your Bonsai. Practice on common garden plants if you're apprehensive about making cuts on your Bonsai.

Understand the Importance of soil and fertilization

Different Bonsai species require different soil mixes for optimal drainage and nutrient retention. Learn about the fertilizers you should use and the appropriate feeding schedule for your Bonsai.

Learn from your mistakes

Everyone makes mistakes, and Bonsai care is no different. Learn from them, and don't be too hard on yourself. Each error offers an opportunity to understand your Bonsai better and improve your skill set.

By taking these steps to learn the essentials about Bonsai, you're laying a solid foundation for your journey. This groundwork will help you make informed decisions as you choose and care for your Bonsai and enhance the enjoyment of your new hobby. With time, care, and ongoing learning, your understanding and appreciation for Bonsai will continue to grow.

Step 7: Financial Investment

The financial commitment to maintaining a Bonsai can vary widely depending on several factors, such as the tree species, the stage of development, and the level of interest you wish to invest. Here are some tips to help you understand and manage the financial aspects of this fulfilling hobby.

Start with a budget

Decide how much you are willing to spend. Bonsai can range from affordable to quite expensive, especially as you get into older, more mature specimens. Set a realistic budget that reflects your level of commitment without putting undue stress on your finances.

Consider older vs. younger trees

Older, more established Bonsai tend to be more expensive. As a beginner, you might opt for a younger tree or even a 'pre-Bonsai,' which is often more cost-effective. These younger trees allow you to learn and make mistakes without a significant financial loss.

DIY to save

If budget is a concern, learn to make your own soil mixes and fertilizer blends. Pre-packaged mixes usually come at a premium, but many recipes can be found online that are less expensive if you source the components separately.

Reuse and recycle

Pots can be among the more expensive items. Look for second-hand or discounted pots, or consider upcycling interesting containers into Bonsai pots. Ensure they have proper drainage and suit the size of your Bonsai.

Buy only necessary tools

Bonsai tools are specialized. Start with an essential Bonsai toolkit and add tools as you develop your skills and require more advanced equipment.

Look for deals

Nurseries offer end-of-season sales, and online markets offer opportunities to buy used Bonsai tools and trees at a lower cost. Look for these deals, but make sure to scrutinize the health and quality of any discounted Bonsai plants.

Invest time, not just money

Remember, investing time in learning proper care techniques can save you money in the long-run by avoiding costly mistakes.

Don't rush into buying

Take your time researching prices and options for buying Bonsai trees and supplies. It's easy to get carried away, so consider each purchase carefully.

By carefully planning your financial investment in Bonsai, you can enjoy the art without it becoming a financial burden. Starting slowly, learning as much as possible, and increasing your investment gradually can help you grow in the hobby financially and experientially.

Step 8: Patience Level

Bonsai is an art that teaches patience through observation and care of a living plant. It's essential to enter this hobby with a clear understanding of the patience required. Here are some suggestions to help you gauge your patience level and how it fits with the practice of Bonsai.

Reflect on your lifestyle

Think about your current hobbies and interests. Do they require patience and attention to detail? How do you feel about activities that show results over months or years rather than immediately? Your answers will give you an insight into whether you'll enjoy the slow pace of Bonsai cultivation.

Start with something simple

Begin with a Bonsai that's known for being hardy and forgiving of novices' mistakes, like a Ficus or Jade plant. A Bonsai that grows more rapidly and can bounce back easily might be better suited to someone cultivating patience.

Set realistic expectations

Understand that Bonsai is not a quick hobby. Trees grow and change slowly, and some styles can take years to achieve. If you're okay with that, you'll find Bonsai to be incredibly rewarding.

Monitor your progress

Keep a journal of your Bonsai's development. This can help you see changes that you might otherwise miss day to day. Over time, you can look back and see just how far your Bonsai has come.

Appreciate the process

Try to find enjoyment in your Bonsai's daily care. Watering, pruning, and simply watching your tree can be calming and meditative acts, each contributing to the overall health and beauty of your Bonsai.

Learn to anticipate

Educate yourself on your tree's growth patterns and seasonal changes. Anticipating and observing these changes can be exciting and make the lengthy process seem faster.

Practice makes patience

If you're naturally impatient, consider Bonsai as a practice to develop more patience. Start with a more resilient tree that won't be too stressed by a missed watering or two, giving you time to integrate Bonsai care into your routine comfortably.

Celebrate small victories

Enjoy the small successes along the way, like the first new leaf or the mastering of a new pruning technique. Recognizing these moments helps cultivate a patient mindset.

Allocate time for Bonsai

Designate a specific time each day or week for Bonsai care. This regular commitment can help establish a routine and make the slow pace of growth feel like part of a bigger picture of consistent care and interaction.

Remember, everyone's patience level varies, and Bonsai offers diverse experiences for different temperaments. Bonsai is not just about cultivating trees but also about cultivating inner calm and a patient perspective, which can benefit all areas of life. By embracing Bonsai's slow and steady nature, you'll grow beautiful trees and nurture a more patient self.

Step 9: Joining the community

Diving into Bonsai can be much more fulfilling when you're part of a community. Not only can you learn from others' experiences, but you can also share your journey and find camaraderie among fellow enthusiasts. Here are some suggestions to help you decide about joining a Bonsai community, along with examples of communities in the USA.

Why join a community?

One of the most significant benefits of joining a community is the wealth of knowledge on offer. From care tips to styling advice, the collective wisdom can be invaluable, especially when just starting out.

Support and encouragement

Sometimes things don't go as planned, and having a support network can keep you motivated. Seasoned members can offer encouragement and tips for overcoming hurdles.

Networking and events

Communities often know about local Bonsai events, exhibits, or workshops. These gatherings can be great opportunities to see a variety of Bonsai styles and meet industry experts.

Friendships and exchange

Bonsai enthusiasts tend to be a passionate bunch, and these communities can lead to lasting friendships. They can also be a place to exchange trees, cuttings, or supplies.

Service and volunteering

Many communities engage in service projects that can enhance your skills while contributing to the group's efforts.

Considerations before joining

Before joining a community, consider if you prefer online interaction or in-person meetings. Also, think about how active you want to be. Can you attend regular meetings or events, or would you prefer a community with a strong online presence that allows participation at your leisure?

Examples of Bonsai Communities in the USA

1. American Bonsai Society (ABS). The ABS is one of America's oldest Bonsai associations, offering a quarterly magazine, conventions, and educational resources. Their website provides information on local clubs throughout the USA.

2. Bonsai Clubs International (BCI). BCI is a non-profit organization

that aims to promote and improve international knowledge and appreciation of Bonsai and related arts. Although it's international, it has a comprehensive list of associated clubs and events across the United States.

3. Local Bonsai Clubs. Almost every state in the USA has local Bonsai clubs, which are often the best places to connect with nearby enthusiasts. Clubs like the Golden State Bonsai Federation in California or the Midwest Bonsai Society in Illinois hold regular exhibit meetings and offer mentorship opportunities.

Getting involved

Start with attending a meeting or event without any obligation to join. Many groups welcome visitors and are happy to share their knowledge with someone just browsing. You can also try multiple clubs to find the right fit for you.

Joining a Bonsai community can enhance your Bonsai experience, providing education, support, and friendship. Whether you choose a local club or an online group, being part of a community of like-minded individuals can be rewarding and can help you grow as a Bonsai artist. Remember, the connection with fellow enthusiasts is as important as with your trees.

Step 10: Goal Setting

Setting clear goals can help guide your journey and enhance your experience with Bonsai. Here are some suggestions designed to help you as a beginner establish goals for your Bonsai tree that will leave you smiling with a sense of accomplishment.

Start with vision

Begin by imagining what you want your Bonsai to look like in the future. Are you aiming for a specific style or shape? Having a vision provides direction for your care and training efforts. It's okay if this vision evolves, as long as it gives you a starting point.

Set short-term goals

Break down your vision into achievable short-term goals. This could be learning to water properly, mastering basic pruning techniques, or simply keeping your Bonsai alive and healthy for the first six months. These incremental goals can provide quick wins and keep you motivated.

Focus on learning

As a beginner, an important goal can be to deepen your understanding of Bonsai. This might include reading one Bonsai book per month, attending workshops, or learning about different soil compositions. By prioritizing education, you'll be better equipped to meet your long-term aspirations.

Plan for each season

Your tree will have different needs throughout the year. Set seasonal goals to learn and perform timely tasks, such as winterizing your Bonsai, adjusting watering schedules for summer, or repotting in the spring.

Track your progress

Documenting your progress can be immensely satisfying. Take photos, keep a journal, or even blog about your Bonsai experience. This record not only serves as motivation but also as a valuable reference.

Incorporate experimentation

Don't be afraid to experiment. Trying new techniques or styles, within reason, can be a goal that leads to greater creativity and understanding. Learn the rules first, so you know how to bend them properly.

Stay flexible

Be prepared to adjust your goals as you gain experience and as your tree develops. Flexibility can help you respond to unexpected challenges and changes with your Bonsai.

Manage expectations

Be kind to yourself and manage your expectations. Not all goals will be met on the first try, and that's perfectly okay. Bonsai is a journey, not a race.

By setting clear, achievable goals and being open to learning, you can progress in the art of Bonsai with a sense of purpose and joy. Remember to smile and enjoy the journey; each step with your Bonsai is a continuous and ever-evolving dance with nature.

CHAPTER 7

Other important decisions

As you step into the delicate world of Bonsai, beyond selecting and caring for your tree, you'll encounter a spectrum of important decisions. Each choice, from the kind of equipment you use to the pots that cradle your trees, contributes to your Bonsai's health and the satisfaction you'll derive from this art form.

Choosing equipment

Entering the Bonsai practice means equipping yourself with the right tools, which will become an extension of your hands and an integral part of your routine care. The equipment you select should be functional, durable, and suitable for the tasks ahead.

Begin with the essentials and choose high-quality tools that will last. Good craftsmanship can make a world of difference in precision, ease of use, and ultimately, your Bonsai's health. Start with a pair of high-quality Bonsai scissors or shears, which are indispensable for pruning leaves and small branches. Bonsai wire cutters are designed to snip wire without damaging the tree, a critical aspect when you're shaping and training your Bonsai. A small hand rake is helpful for working the soil during re-potting and a pair of tweezers for detail work and removal of debris.

As you become more engrossed in Bonsai, specialty tools like knob cutters for removing protrusions, and root hooks for detangling roots during repotting, can be valuable additions. Concave branch cutters allow for precise cuts that heal smoothly on the tree. For convenience, consider purchasing a Bonsai toolkit. These kits typically include the basic tools in a handy case, ensuring that you have everything you need to get started.

Remember that your tools need care, too. Keep them clean and dry to prevent rust and disease spreading between plants. Sharpening your tools regularly keeps them effective and makes them easier to use.

Be conscious of your Bonsai's scale. If you are managing a small Bonsai, heavy or large equipment may be cumbersome. Conversely, larger trees require sturdier tools that can handle thicker branches.

Approaching equipment choice with care will pay off in the long run and enhance your Bonsai practice. Quality equipment performs better and brings a greater sense of joy and accomplishment to the Bonsai experience.

Choosing pots

Selecting the right pot for your Bonsai is not just about aesthetics; it's a crucial decision that affects the health and growth of your tree. Here are some suggestions to help you choose a good pot for your first tree.

The pot should be in proportion to your tree. A general rule of thumb is that the pot's length should be roughly two-thirds the height of your tree. For width, the pot should be just a little wider than the spread of the branches. The depth should coordinate with the diameter of the trunk; a thicker trunk requires a deeper pot, but it shouldn't be so deep as to drown the roots.

Pots come in various materials like ceramic, plastic, or even concrete. For beginners, a ceramic pot is a durable choice that offers good aesthetics and functionality. However, they can be more expensive and heavier than plastic pots, which are lighter and less fragile.

Good drainage is essential to prevent water from pooling and causing root rot. Ensure the pot has adequate drainage holes. Some pots also have tie-down holes to secure the Bonsai in place. Choose a pot that complements your tree without overshadowing it. The color and texture should not distract from the Bonsai. Earthy, muted tones are typically a safe bet for most tree species. Also, consider the tree's style when choosing a pot shape—oval or rectangular pots suit most tree styles, whereas round pots can enhance the symmetry of flowering or fruiting Bonsai.

Your first pot should be durable to withstand repotting as your Bonsai grows. Avoid overly delicate pots that may crack or chip easily during routine care. Your Bonsai might fit snugly into the pot now, it's wise to consider its growth potential. However, avoid a pot that's too large, as this can make watering and nutrient intake inefficient for the tree.

If you live in a region with severe weather changes, a heavier pot can provide stability against strong winds, and a high-fired ceramic pot can resist frost damage.

Remember, the pot is both the home and the frame for your Bonsai, and making a thoughtful choice for this critical component can enhance your Bonsai's beauty and contribute to a healthy, happy tree.

Choosing soil

The soil you choose for your Bonsai is crucial, serving as the main source of nutrition and support for your tree. Here are some suggestions on selecting the best soil for your first Bonsai. Bonsai soil is a mix of components that provide drainage, aeration, and water retention. A common mix includes akadama, pumice, and lava rock. Akadama is a clay-like mineral that helps retain water; pumice aids in aeration and moisture regulation; and lava rock contributes to drainage and structure.

For beginners, pre-mixed Bonsai soils are a great starting point. These are specifically formulated to provide a balance suitable for a wide range of Bonsai trees and remove the guesswork from having to mix your own.

Different species of Bonsai require different soil requirements. Research what soil mixture is best suited for your tree's type. Deciduous trees often flourish in soil that retains more moisture, while succulents and pines prefer a well-draining mix. Ensuring your soil provides proper drainage is paramount. Overly dense soil can lead to waterlogging, root rot, and ultimately, the death of your tree. Your soil should allow water to move freely while still holding enough to keep roots moist.

As you become more experienced, you may wish to customize your soil mix to suit your tree's specific needs and your local climate. Adjusting the components and their ratios can optimize the balance between water retention and drainage. Some Bonsai trees prefer a particular soil pH range. Buying a pH testing kit can help you maintain the right level for your tree, which affects nutrient uptake.

While it's tempting to cut corners with cheaper soil options, good-quality soil is an investment in your Bonsai's health. Cheap potting soil often lacks the necessary qualities for Bonsai and can compact over time, suffocating the roots.

Avoid Garden Soil

Garden or yard soil generally isn't suitable for Bonsai. It can compact in pots, lacks proper drainage, and may contain pests or diseases.

Remember, while good-quality soil can seem like a small detail, it's actually the lifeblood of your Bonsai. Providing your tree with the proper foundation will encourage healthy growth and allow you to enjoy the beauty of Bonsai for many years to come.

FAQ:

Why is it important to avoid using garden soil for Bonsai?

There are several reasons why it's crucial to avoid using garden soil for Bonsai:

Drainage: Garden soil tends to compact, especially when put in a small pot, which can hinder water drainage. Bonsai need soil that allows water to flow through easily to prevent root rot and other water-related diseases.

Aeration: Healthy root growth requires soil that provides good aeration. Compacted garden soil can suffocate the roots, restricting the oxygen supply vital for the tree's health and growth.

Pests and Diseases: Garden soil could contain pests, fungi, or disease microorganisms that might be hard to control once introduced to the Bonsai environment and could potentially harm or even kill your Bonsai.

Nutrient Balance: Garden soil may not provide the optimal balance of nutrients required for Bonsai. Bonsai trees often have specific nutritional needs, which are generally met with specialized Bonsai soil mixes.

pH Level: The pH of garden soil may not be suitable for Bonsai. Some Bonsai species thrive in specific pH levels, and using garden soil could throw off this balance, affecting the tree's ability to absorb essential nutrients.

Choosing decorations

Decorations, when used thoughtfully, can enhance the appeal of your Bonsai display and give your little tree its own unique landscape. Here are some suggestions to choose good decorations for your first Bonsai.

Aim for decorations that mimic natural elements and blend

harmoniously with your tree. Rocks, mosses, small figurines that represent animals, or even tiny huts can add a sense of environment. Be careful not to clutter; decorations should complement, not overwhelm. Select decorations that maintain the illusion of your Bonsai being a full-size tree. This means choosing items that are in scale with the size of your Bonsai so as not to disrupt the miniature landscape you're creating.

Consider adding elements that correspond with the current season to make the scene more dynamic. For instance, you might add a carpet of bright moss or blooming miniatures to signify spring. Items that suit the specific style (informal upright, cascade, etc.) and species of your Bonsai will create a cohesive look. A rock might complement the rugged appearance of a pine, while a small bench figurine may pair nicely with a flowering cherry tree.

Opt for high-quality, durable materials that can withstand the conditions your Bonsai is in, especially if it's an outdoor tree. Natural stones, for example, can weather the elements better than painted plastics. Start with fewer items and let the beauty of your Bonsai stand forefront. It's easy to over-decorate; simplicity often leads to elegance.

Don't hesitate to try different decorations to see what looks best but be willing to remove items that don't work. The beauty of Bonsai is in its change and evolution, and this extends to your choice of decorations.

Incorporating these guidelines while selecting your Bonsai decorations allows you to create a personalized and aesthetically pleasing miniature landscape that enhances the viewing pleasure of your Bonsai tree.

FAQ:

What natural elements can be used as decorations for a Bonsai tree?

For decorating your Bonsai, incorporating natural elements can really tie your miniature landscape to the broader natural world and imbue it with a touch of realism. Here are some natural elements you can consider:

Moss: Adding moss around the base of your Bonsai can give the appearance of a lawn or underbrush, making your tree seem larger by comparison. Plus, moss helps retain soil moisture.

Rocks and Stones: Rocks can mimic mountains or cliffs when placed thoughtfully around your Bonsai. They add a sense of age and permanence to your composition.

Gravel or Sand: They can create pathways or symbolize water bodies, leading to a serene and well-balanced scene.

Miniature Plants: Small groundcovers or plants that mimic shrubs can complement the tree without overshadowing it. Choose species that can thrive in the same conditions as your Bonsai.

Deadwood: Pieces of driftwood or dead branches that are properly sanitized can simulate fallen logs or natural woodland debris.

Water Features: If you're feeling more ambitious and have the right setup, a small water dish can resemble a lake or pond, adding tranquility to your Bonsai landscape.

Remember to choose appropriately sized elements to maintain the illusion of scale in your Bonsai display, and always make sure any added natural materials are clean and free from pests or disease.

What about fertilizer?

Fertilizer is essential to provide your Bonsai with the nutrients it needs to thrive, especially since it's growing in a limited amount of soil. Here are suggestions to help you choose the right fertilizer for your first tree.

Most fertilizers come with three key nutrients listed as NPK: Nitrogen (N) for foliage growth, Phosphorus (P) for roots and flowers, and Potassium (K) for overall health. Look for a balanced fertilizer like a 10-10-10 or a specific formula suited for the type of Bonsai you have.

Young, actively growing Bonsai may benefit from a higher nitrogen content to promote growth. In contrast, for an established Bonsai where size is being maintained, a balanced or even low-nitrogen fertilizer may be more suitable.

Granular fertilizers release nutrients slowly and need to be applied less frequently. Liquid fertilizers are absorbed quickly but require more frequent applications. For beginners, liquid fertilizers can be easier to manage and adjust based on the tree's response.

Organic fertilizers, like fish emulsion or cottonseed meal, release nutrients slowly and can improve soil health over time. They're often less concentrated than synthetic fertilizers, reducing the risk of over-fertilization. Read the label for recommendations on how often to apply.

Generally, you should fertilize during the growing season, cutting back in the winter when the tree is dormant. Over-fertilizing can harm your Bonsai, so it's better to err on the side of caution, especially when starting out.

Every tree is different. Start with a recommended dose and observe your Bonsai's reaction over time, adjusting as necessary. If the tree appears healthy and is growing as expected, you're probably on the right track.

There are fertilizers specifically made for Bonsai that take the guesswork out of NPK ratios. These can be a great starting point for beginners to ensure their trees receive a balanced diet. Always water your tree before applying fertilizer. This prevents the roots from burning and helps the nutrients disperse evenly through the soil.

Choosing the right fertilizer and applying it correctly can make a significant difference in the health and appearance of your Bonsai. It supports vigorous growth and helps in the development of a strong and beautiful miniature tree. Remember to always follow product instructions and watch how your Bonsai responds to find the best fertilizer regimen.

FAQ:

What are the advantages of using organic fertilizers for Bonsai trees?

Organic fertilizers offer several advantages for Bonsai trees. Here are some of the benefits:

1. Slow Nutrient Release: Organic fertilizers generally break down and release nutrients slowly as they are decomposed by soil organisms. This means there's less risk of overfeeding and burning the roots, which is particularly important in the confined space of a Bonsai pot.

2. Improved Soil Structure: The organic matter in these fertilizers improves soil aeration and water retention, which helps Bonsai roots grow and absorb nutrients efficiently.

3. Beneficial Soil Organisms: Organic fertilizers support a healthy and diverse soil ecosystem by providing food for beneficial microorganisms. These organisms help break down the organic matter into nutrients that the Bonsai can use.

4. Natural Ingredients: Organic fertilizers are made from natural materials such as fish emulsion, bone meal, or composted manure, so they are less likely to introduce harmful chemicals into your Bonsai's environment.

5. Environmental Friendliness: Organic fertilizers are more environmentally friendly because they are renewable and biodegradable, reducing the chemical load on the environment.

6. Encourages Strong Growth: While they may not produce the rapid growth spurts seen with synthetic fertilizers, organic options promote steady and robust growth that is more in line with the natural growth patterns Bonsai enthusiasts often prefer.

7. Reduced Leaching: Since nutrients from organic fertilizers are released slowly, they are less likely to leach out of the soil and into the water table, making them a more sustainable option for nutrient delivery.

When choosing fertilizers, consider the specific needs of your Bonsai and the characteristics of the organic options available to ensure your miniature tree gets the best possible care.

What tools do you need?

When you're just starting with Bonsai, having the right tools can make all the difference. Here's a list of essential tools for Bonsai care, along with suggestions for choosing good ones for your first tree.

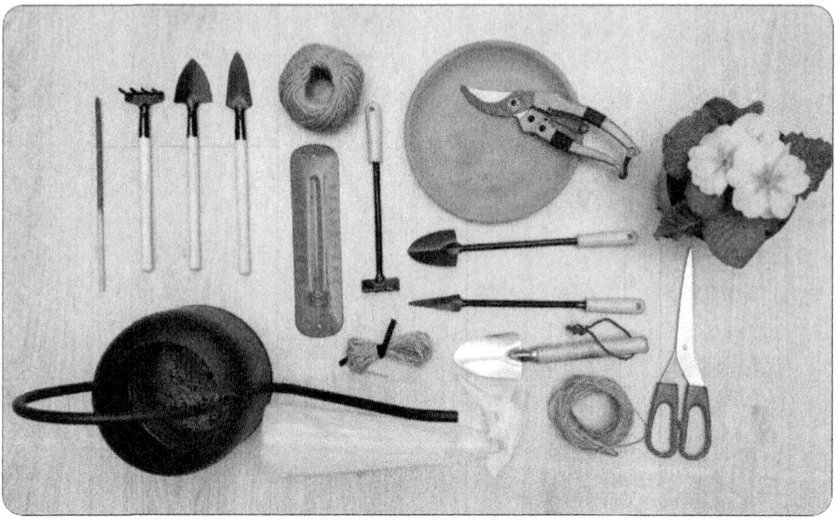

Picture 13: Basic tools, image: Freepik.com.

Pruning Shears: These are probably the most frequently used tools. Look for a sharp, high-quality pair made of stainless steel for precision cuts that will heal quickly.

Concave Branch Cutters: These cutters leave a hollow, concave cut that heals with the least amount of scarring. Choose one made from durable materials to handle the removal of branches.

Wire Cutters: Specifically designed for Bonsai, these ensure that you can cut the wire without damaging the tree. Invest in a pair that's able to cut both thin and thick wires with ease.

Bonsai Scissors: For trimming leaves and fine branches, a good pair of Bonsai scissors is indispensable. Their short, sharp blades make precise cuts and are designed to be comfortable to use for extended periods.

Root Rake: This tool helps to untangle roots during repotting without causing too much damage. A sturdy, stainless steel rake can be a good choice for beginners.

Knob Cutters: These are used to cut through thick branches and knobs while leaving a smooth surface. Look for knob cutters that feel solid and fit comfortably in your hand.

Tweezers: High-grade stainless steel tweezers can help with removing dead leaves or insects and are useful for delicate adjustments to the placement of foliage or wiring.

Bonsai Wire: To shape and train branches, you'll need various thicknesses of wire. Aluminum wire is easier to bend and is often recommended for beginners.

Soil Scoop: A small scoop is very handy for repotting. It helps in adding and removing soil in the pot. Opt for a durable scoop that fits comfortably in your hand.

When starting, consider purchasing a Bonsai tool kit, which often includes the basic tools at a more economical price than buying them individually. As you grow in the hobby, you can add higher-quality or more specialized tools to your collection. Remember, keeping your tools clean and properly stored will extend their life and make your Bonsai care that much more enjoyable.

FAQ:

What are the benefits of using pruning shears for Bonsai care?

Using pruning shears for Bonsai care offers significant benefits, contributing immensely to the health and aesthetics of the tree:

Precision in Pruning: Pruning shears are designed to make clean, precise cuts, which is essential for shaping Bonsai trees without causing unnecessary damage to the branches.

Promoting Healthy Growth: Good pruning practices help direct growth by removing unnecessary shoots or leaves. This not only improves the tree's appearance but also ensures that nutrients are directed to the parts of the tree where they are most needed.

Disease Prevention: Pruning away dead or diseased foliage with shears can prevent the spread of disease and pests, keeping the Bonsai healthy.

Size and Scale Maintenance: Pruning helps maintain the miniature scale of a Bonsai, ensuring that it doesn't outgrow its design or pot.

Aesthetics: Pruning shears allow the artist to sculpt the Bonsai into desired styles and forms, creating a visually pleasing miniature landscape.

Quick Healing: Using clean and sharp pruning shears makes cuts that heal faster than torn or jagged ones. This is crucial for the tree's recovery and continued growth.

Ultimately, pruning shears are an indispensable tool in the art of Bonsai and, when used correctly, they are key to cultivating a beautiful and thriving Bonsai.

CHAPTER 8

Why might the Bonsai tree die?

L ike all living plants, bonsai trees have requirements that can be overlooked. Here are some common reasons why a Bonsai might die and suggestions to prevent such a loss.

Improper watering

Overwatering can lead to root rot while underwatering can dry out the tree.

To prevent this: Use a well-draining soil mix to prevent water from pooling around the roots. Develop a consistent watering routine, making adjustments based on the season and the tree's needs. Check the soil moisture before watering; it should be slightly damp, not completely dry or soaked.

Incorrect light

Too much or too little light can stress the tree. To ensure proper light: Research the specific light requirements for your Bonsai species. Place your Bonsai in a location where it will receive the appropriate amount of sunlight. Use grow lights if natural light is insufficient, particularly during winter months.

Pests and diseases

Infestations can sicken or kill a Bonsai. To protect your tree: Inspect regularly for signs of pests or disease. Quarantine new plants before introducing them to your collection. Use appropriate treatments like insecticidal soaps or neem oil, but always follow the instructions and test on a small area first.

Lack of nutrition

Bonsai trees need regular feeding to avoid malnutrition. During the growing season, Fertilize with an appropriate Bonsai fertilizer and adjust feeding to the tree's growth stages and seasonal needs.

Environmental stress

Sudden changes in temperature or location can shock a Bonsai. To minimize stress: Protect outdoor Bonsai from extreme temperatures with appropriate shelter or by bringing them indoors when necessary. Avoid placing your Bonsai in locations with direct heat sources or drafts from air conditioning and heaters.

Poor pruning practices

Incorrect pruning can introduce disease or weaken the tree. To prune properly: Sterilize your pruning tools before each use. Learn proper pruning techniques specific to your Bonsai species. Avoid over-pruning; your tree needs enough foliage to photosynthesize effectively.

Substandard soil

Using garden soil or an unsuitable mix can suffocate roots and hinder water drainage. To prevent soil issues: Use a specialized Bonsai soil mix with good drainage and aeration. Replace the soil every few years, or as recommended for your tree, to refresh nutrient content and improve soil structure.

Remember, Bonsai care is a learning experience, and sometimes, it takes a few tries to get it right. By understanding your Bonsai's needs and providing attentive care, you can greatly improve its chances of thriving for many years to come.

CHAPTER 9

TOP 5 plants for a beginner

E mbarking on an indoor Bonsai journey can be exciting and rewarding. Here are the top five plants suitable for beginners and why these choices can lead to a successful start in Bonsai.

1. Ficus Bonsai (Ficus retusa / Ficus ginseng): The Ficus is incredibly tolerant of indoor conditions. It's flexible when it comes to light, watering, and humidity, making it a forgiving option for beginners. Its robust nature and ability to survive in less than perfect conditions make the Ficus a staple in the indoor Bonsai world. Ficus Bonsai also have the capacity to produce aerial roots, which add to their exotic appeal.

Picture 14: Ficus Bonsai (Ficus retusa / Ficus ginseng).

Suitability: Best for those who are looking for a hardy species that responds well to indoor environments and are maybe also dealing with less-than-ideal lighting conditions.

2. Chinese Elm (Ulmus parvifolia): Chinese Elm is a versatile and hardy tree that adapts well to the indoor climate and is also quite forgiving. It has a beautiful, intricate twig structure, small leaves, and a forgiving nature regarding watering and light conditions.

Picture 15: Chinese Elm (Ulmus parvifolia).

Suitability: Ideal for those who appreciate a classic Bonsai appearance and might have varying conditions in their home throughout the year.

3. Jade Plant (Crassula ovata): The Jade Plant is a succulent that makes a good indoor Bonsai. It's very easy to care for, requiring little water and tolerating a wide range of light conditions. Its thick trunk and glossy green leaves give it a mature, tree-like appearance.

Picture 16: Jade Plant (Crassula ovata).

Suitability: Suitable for forgetful gardeners as it copes well with sporadic watering. It's also perfect for sunny locations.

4. Sweet Plum (Sageretia theezans): Also known as the Chinese Bird Plum, this Bonsai features small leaves and a stunning gnarled trunk. It's quite tolerant of indoor conditions and pruning, which encourages a bushy growth habit.

Picture 17: Sweet Plum (Sageretia theezans).

Suitability: Great for those who enjoy shaping their Bonsai, as it responds well to pruning and wiring techniques.

5. Dwarf Schefflera (Schefflera arboricola): The Dwarf Schefflera can be easily grown indoors. Its resilience to lower light and ability to withstand some dryness makes it a practical choice for beginners. This species can also develop interesting aerial roots.

Picture 18: Dwarf Schefflera (Schefflera arboricola).

Suitability: A fitting choice for individuals living in homes with less natural light or for those who travel frequently and need a Bonsai that can tolerate a missed watering.

What trees are suitable for you?

To choose the right tree for you, consider your home environment and the conditions you can provide. Temperature fluctuations, light levels, humidity, and your personal schedule should all factor into your decision. Start with these forgiving species, learn as you go, and soon you'll gain the confidence to try more challenging Bonsai trees.

CHAPTER 10

How to get your tree?

C hoosing and buying your first Bonsai tree is an important step in starting your Bonsai journey. Here are some suggestions on how to get your tree and where to look for one.

Local Bonsai Nurseries: Visit a local Bonsai nursery if you have one. This is ideal because you can see the trees in person, and the staff can provide valuable advice on the care of the Bonsai. The trees are likely already acclimated to your local climate.

Gardening Centers: Many garden centers and nurseries have a section for Bonsai. While the staff may not be as specialized as at a Bonsai nursery, they can still offer general guidance.

Specialty Bonsai Shops: Specialty shops often have a wider selection, including starter kits ideal for beginners. Shop owners can be a wealth of knowledge and provide personalized advice.

Online Retailers: Purchasing a Bonsai online can be convenient and sometimes necessary if local options are limited. Look for reputable online stores with good reviews and ensure a safe delivery guarantee.

Bonsai Exhibitions or Shows: Bonsai shows not only display trees but often have sales areas. These can be a great opportunity to purchase high-quality trees and meet local experts.

Bonsai Clubs or Societies: Members sometimes sell trees or may know of good local sources where beginners can purchase Bonsai. Some clubs also hold auctions or sales.

Things to Consider When Buying Your First Tree

Health: Look for a tree with vibrant foliage and no signs of pests or diseases.

Structure: Choose a tree with a good branch structure and potential for development.

Species: Pick a species that suits your climate and indoor conditions, especially if you cannot provide specialized care.

Budget: Set a budget beforehand, as prices can vary widely based on the age and species of the tree.

Support: Ideally, buy from a source where ongoing support and advice are available, especially when starting.

When buying your first Bonsai, take your time to choose a tree that resonates with you and fits your living environment. This initial choice can set the tone for your Bonsai experience, so it's worth making sure you choose wisely.

Buy or start from seed?

We have already discussed this issue above. And I strongly recommended that you buy a ready-made tree rather than grow it from seed. But here are a few more arguments in favor of buying a finished tree.

Buying a tree rather than starting from seed allows for a quicker start, as seeds can take years to reach a stage suitable for Bonsai styling. When purchasing an established tree, you can immediately practice Bonsai techniques and enjoy a mature appearance much sooner. It also lets you select a tree with desirable traits and structure, ensuring a certain level of predictability in your Bonsai's development.

An older Bonsai will often be more forgiving and resilient to careless mistakes for beginners than a young, fragile seedling. Buying a tree provides immediate gratification—a small but complete Bonsai you can display and enjoy from day one.

What is essential when you choose the tree?

Health: Look for a tree with a healthy appearance—vibrant leaves or needles, firm bark, and no signs of pests or disease.

Structure: A well-structured trunk with good branch placement allows for more styling options and a more aesthetically pleasing Bonsai in the long run.

Root System: A strong, well-distributed root system is crucial for the tree's stability and health. If possible, check that the roots are not girdling or excessively tangled.

Species Suitability: Ensure the species is suited to your local climate if it will be kept outdoors and your home environment if it's an indoor Bonsai.

Personal Connection: Choose a tree that speaks to you, one that you're drawn to. This personal connection will make the care and time you invest in it more enjoyable.

Tips for buying a quality tree

When buying a quality Bonsai tree, keep these main tips in mind:

1. Examine the Tree: Look closely at the overall health, including the leaves, trunk, and roots. The tree should be free of pests, diseases, and any noticeable damage.

2. Assess the Trunk: A good Bonsai will have a strong and interesting trunk, often with a thicker base, which gives the tree a sense of age and stability.

3. Check Branch Structure: Well-placed and proportionate branches are crucial for future styling. Branches should decrease in size and quantity as they ascend.

4. Root Health: Healthy roots are essential. They should not be circling excessively, which can indicate they are pot-bound, and the visible surface roots (nebari) should be well distributed.

5. Pot Match: Ensure the pot is appropriate for the tree in terms of size, style, and drainage. It should complement the tree without distracting from it.

6. Soil Condition: The Bonsai should be planted in a suitable soil mix that allows for proper drainage and aeration.

7. Species Research: Know the specifics of the species you're considering and ensure it's suitable for your climate and care capacity.

How to deliver it to home correctly?

After purchasing your first Bonsai tree, delivering it safely to your home is a crucial step to ensure its continued health. Here's how to do it correctly:

1. Steady Temperature: Try to maintain a consistent temperature during transport, avoiding extremes by using your car's heating or cooling as necessary.

2. Secure Positioning: Place your Bonsai in a stable position in your vehicle to prevent it from tipping over. Using a box or a container to surround the pot can help, and if the tree is small, it might be placed in a cup holder for added security.

3. Minimize Movement: To minimize movement and possible

damage, cushion the area around the pot with soft materials such as towels, bubble wrap, or newspapers.

4. Avoid Direct Sunlight: In the car, avoid leaving the Bonsai in direct sunlight for extended periods as this can overheat the tree and dry out the soil.

5. Drive Carefully: Take turns and stops gently to prevent jostling the tree too much.

6. Acclimate Gradually: Once home, allow your tree to acclimate gradually to its new environment.

Don't place it immediately in bright sunlight or at a temperature very different from what it experienced in its previous location.

FAQ:

How can I protect my Bonsai tree from direct sunlight during transportation?

Protecting your Bonsai from direct sunlight during transportation is key to preventing heat stress and dehydration. Here are some steps to ensure safe transit:

Shade the Tree: Use a lightweight, breathable material, like a cotton cloth or a shade net, to cover your Bonsai. Ensure it's loose enough not to damage the foliage but effective in blocking direct sunlight.

Use Car Sunshades: If transporting by car, employ window sunshades to reflect sunlight away from the interior where the Bonsai is placed.

Positioning Inside Vehicle: Keep the Bonsai on the floor of the car, preferably behind the front seats or in the trunk, where it is less likely to be exposed to direct sunlight through the windows.

Time Your Travel: If possible, travel during cooler parts of the day, such as early morning or late afternoon, when the sun isn't at its peak intensity.

Tinted Windows: If your vehicle has tinted windows that block UV rays, use these to your advantage to provide additional protection.

Ventilation: Ensure good air circulation in the vehicle to prevent heat build-up which can accompany direct sunlight exposure.

With these precautions, you can prevent sun damage and provide a safe journey for your Bonsai tree.

CHAPTER 11

Your first Bonsai tree

A t this point, you already know enough to select and purchase your first Bonsai tree. Let's say you've already made a purchase and brought the tree home. What's next?

Picture 19: Bonsai trees in Yose-Ue style. (Rustling leaves - Silence in the forest)

Repotting immediately or wait a little?

When you bring a new Bonsai tree home, it's generally best to wait a bit before repotting. Give your tree some time to acclimatize to its new surroundings first. This adjustment period could range from a few weeks to the end of the current growing season, depending on the health of the tree and the time of year.

However, if you notice pressing issues, such as soil that doesn't drain properly, signs of root rot, or if the tree is dangerously pot-bound, then you may need to repot sooner for the health of the tree. If this is the case, proceed with caution and make sure you've researched the specific needs and proper repotting procedure for your Bonsai species.

As a general rule though, if the tree seems healthy, repotting can wait until the recommended season, which is typically early spring as the tree comes out of dormancy.

Where to put the tree in the first couple of days?

In the first couple of days after you bring your Bonsai home, you should place the tree in a location where it will be protected from extreme temperatures and direct sunlight to prevent stress.

Opt for a spot with bright, indirect light and stable temperature conditions. This might be near a bright window with a sheer curtain or in an area that gets filtered sunlight throughout the day.

Also, keep it away from drafts, heating vents, and air conditioning as these can quickly dry out the foliage. Monitor your tree closely during this time to make sure it's adjusting well to its new environment.

After a few days to a week, when your Bonsai seems to have acclimated, you can gradually move it to its more permanent location as per the specific light and temperature requirements of its species.

Should I place it in the bright sun or not?

This is an interesting question, and one that newbies often make. Let's rephrase the question itself and give a detailed answer.

FAQ:

How long should I wait before exposing my Bonsai tree to direct sunlight after bringing it home?

After bringing your new Bonsai home, it's wise to give it some time to adjust to its new environment before exposing it to direct sunlight. Start with a period of about one to two weeks in a partially shaded area where it can receive plenty of indirect sunlight.

Gradually increase its exposure to direct sunlight over the course of several more weeks, monitoring the tree's response. Keep an eye out for any signs of stress, such as leaf scorching or wilting, which may indicate that the transition is too rapid.

Adjusting your Bonsai to its new setting slowly helps ensure a smooth acclimation process, leading to a healthier and happier tree.

The soil is dry; what should I do?

If the soil of your Bonsai tree feels dry, it might be time to water. Here's a proper watering technique for a Bonsai:

Watering Method: Avoid watering lightly; instead, water thoroughly until water begins to drain from the holes at the bottom of the pot. This ensures that the entire root system gets hydrated.

Water Quality: Preferably use rainwater or tap water that has been left to stand for a while, as they're usually better for the Bonsai than fresh tap water. Avoid using water with a high mineral content like hard water.

Soil Soak: For a very dry Bonsai, you might need to completely immerse the pot in a tub of water for about 5-10 minutes to rehydrate the entire root mass.

Remember, the rule of thumb for watering Bonsai is to check the soil moisture level first. If the top inch of soil feels dry, it's generally time to water. But always take into consideration the specific water requirements of your Bonsai species. It's important not to overwater, as this can lead to root rot and other diseases.

Why is Bonsai more fantastic than pets?

While "fantastic" might be subjective and many people find pets to be incomparable companions, Bonsai trees do have unique attributes that might be deemed more appealing to some individuals:

Tranquility: Bonsai trees offer a sense of peace and serenity, which can be a calming presence in your home.

Artistic Expression: Cultivating Bonsai is an art form that allows personal creative expression by shaping and styling a living tree.

Low Maintenance: Compared to pets, Bonsai trees require less day-to-day care, no walking, and they don't need to be fed multiple times a day.

Longevity: Many Bonsai trees can live for hundreds of years, becoming heirlooms and lasting legacies.

Space Saving: Bonsai occupy very little space, making them suitable for small living areas without the need for outdoor space or exercise.

In either case, whether with Bonsai or pets, the joy and fulfillment they bring to individuals is subjective and based on personal preferences and lifestyles.

CHAPTER 12

Looking after the Bonsai tree

F rom the gentle nuances of watering to the more complex decisions concerning fertilizers, this chapter covers all corners of Bonsai caretaking. We'll delve into the seasonal tasks relevant to spring's awakening, summer's vigor, autumn's preparation, and winter's rest, ensuring you're equipped with the knowledge to support your Bonsai throughout the year.

Whether you're untangling the mysteries of wiring, pondering the timing of your pruning, or learning to shape your tree with an artist's touch, we've curated expert tips and step-by-step tutorials to help your tree reach its full potential. The health of your Bonsai is fundamental, so we've included troubleshooting advice for those peculiar moments and guidance on occasional but critical tasks, such as unwiring and sterilizing tools.

How much water?

The question of how much water your Bonsai tree needs is a vital one, and the answer depends on several factors including the tree species, the size of the tree, the size of the pot, the soil composition, and environmental conditions such as temperature, humidity, and light exposure.

Here's a general guideline:

Check the Soil: Before watering, check the topsoil—about an inch deep—for moisture. If it feels dry, your Bonsai likely needs water.

Water Thoroughly: When it's time to water, do so until water flows out of the drainage holes. This ensures the whole root system is hydrated.

Frequency: Some trees may need watering once a day, while others may only need watering once a week. Observe your tree's response to watering to determine the right frequency.

Seasonal Adjustments: Water more frequently during the growing season (spring and summer) and reduce watering in the dormant season (fall and winter).

Morning Watering: The best time to water is usually in the morning, as this ensures the tree has enough moisture throughout the day when it's actively photosynthesizing.

Watering is both an art and a science, and getting to know the needs of your specific Bonsai tree will ensure it remains healthy and beautiful.

More about fertilizers

Fertilizing your Bonsai tree is key to its health because the limited soil volume can only provide so much nourishment. Here's a breakdown of when to fertilize, how much to use, and what type of fertilizers are suitable.

When to Fertilize: Fertilize during the growing season, which is typically from early spring to late autumn. It's best to avoid fertilizing a sick tree or one that has just been repotted. Additionally, refrain from fertilizing in the height of summer when some Bonsai types go into a period of dormancy due to the heat.

How Much to Fertilize: The quantity will vary depending on the fertilizer type and the size of your Bonsai. Always refer to the instructions provided with your fertilizer. As a general rule, it's better to under-fertilize than over-fertilize, which can lead to root burn and other health issues.

What Type of Fertilizer: There are two main types of fertilizer: organic and chemical (inorganic).

Organic Fertilizers: These are made from natural materials and release nutrients slowly as they break down, which reduces the risk of over-fertilization. Examples include fish emulsion, cottonseed meal, and bone meal.

Chemical Fertilizers: These are man-made and typically come in a balanced formulation like 10-10-10, which represents the ratio of nitrogen, phosphorus, and potassium. They deliver nutrients directly to the tree, which can prompt a faster response.

Fertilizer Form: Fertilizers can come in various forms, such as liquids, granules, or spikes. Liquids are fast-acting, while granules offer a slow-release option. Spikes can be convenient but are less common for Bonsai due to the small pot size.

Remember, the key is to follow a consistent fertilization schedule, adjust as needed based on the tree's response, and ensure you provide the right nutrients for your specific type of Bonsai.

CHAPTER 13

Wiring the Bonsai tree

T his chapter is the most sensitive. You have to master the basics of wiring. Next, I will continue my story about the wonderful world of Bonsai and its aspects.

Basic wiring

Basic wiring is a fundamental technique in Bonsai shaping, allowing you to direct and set the branches of your tree. When done with care and precision, wiring gives you the ability to create a more aesthetically pleasing form in your Bonsai.

Here's how to wire your Bonsai tree properly:

Choose the Right Wire: The wire should be about one-third the thickness of the branch you're wiring. Aluminum wire is commonly used for its flexibility and ease of manipulation; copper wire is also an option, especially for conifers.

Prepare the Tree: Clean off any dead needles or leaves where you'll be applying the wire. Also, ensure the tree is properly hydrated, as this makes the branches more pliable.

Anchoring: Start by anchoring the wire to the trunk or a sturdy, low branch for stability. Wrap the wire around the trunk at a 45-degree angle, making sure it's snug but not digging into the bark.

Wiring Branches: Extend the wire from the anchor point to your chosen branch, keeping the angle consistent. Ensure each coil is neat and equidistant but not constricting the branch.

Directions: When possible, always wire two branches with one piece of wire. This adds stability and helps prevent wire marks on the trunk.

Manipulation: Once the wire is in place, gently bend the branch into the desired shape. Avoid sharp bends, which can snap the branch. Gradual curves are more natural and more accessible to achieve.

Monitoring: After wiring, regularly check the growth of the branches. As the tree grows, the wire can cut into the bark, which can cause damage. The wire should be removed before it starts to scar the branch, usually within a year.

Basic wiring is not something to rush. Take your time, and remember: it's as much about the tree's health and natural growth as it is about achieving a certain look. With practice and patience, wiring will become a comfortable and rewarding part of your Bonsai journey.

Wiring bonsai branches is a careful process that encourages them to grow in certain directions, contributing greatly to the aesthetic appeal of the bonsai. Here's how to wire branches in three steps:

Step 1: Begin with Proper Placement. Start by cutting a length of wire that is long enough to cover the branch you wish to wire, then cut some. It's better to have a little extra wire than not enough. Begin wiring at the branch's base, known as the "shoulder," near where it connects to the trunk. This ensures that the wire is anchored well. As you wrap the wire around the branch, ensure it sits snug against the branch without any gaps, particularly close to the trunk. This placement is crucial because when the branch tries to spring back to its original position after being bent, the wire will obstruct it, effectively holding the branch in its new position.

Step 2: Avoid Incorrect Wiring Techniques. When wiring, especially if you plan to bend the branch downwards, start the wiring at the branch's shoulder rather than at the crotch (where the branch forks or joins the trunk). If you start wiring at the crotch, the wire acts as a pivot point during bending, which puts too much stress on the branch and increases the risk of it breaking. Without the wire snugly placed over the shoulder of the branch, there is a lack of support on the top part of the branch, making it vulnerable to tearing away from the trunk or snapping outright.

Step 3: Maximize Stability with Dual Branch Wiring. It's more effective to wire two branches with a single piece of wire when possible. This approach lends additional stability, as the trunk section between the branches serves as an anchoring point. This technique is especially useful when you want to adjust the direction or angle of two branches near each other. Make sure that the wire wraps over the shoulder for both branches. This way, when you apply force to bend and lower the branches, the wire running over the shoulder of each branch provides a solid hold, significantly reducing the risk of damage.

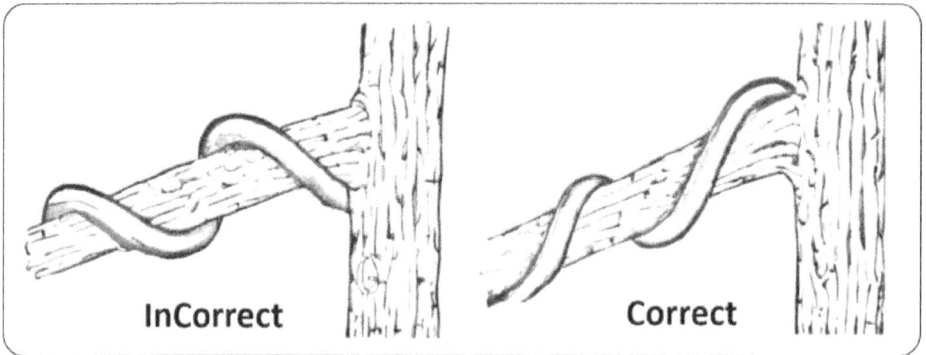

Picture 20: Bonsai Basic Wiring

By following these steps, you ensure the proper shaping of your bonsai's branches and minimize potential harm to the tree during the process. Wiring with care and precision is key to achieving beautiful, healthy bonsai forms.

The ratio of branch thickness to the appropriate thickness of copper wire and aluminum wire can help ensure you're using the right wire for your bonsai shaping needs. It's important to note that, generally, aluminum wire is used at about one-third to one-half the thickness of the branch being wired, whereas copper wire, being stronger, is typically used at about one-quarter to one-third the thickness of the branch.

Here's a simple table to guide you:

Branch Thickness	Copper Wire Thickness	Aluminum Wire Thickness
1/8 inch (3.175 mm)	1/32 inch (0.8 mm)	1/16 inch (1.6 mm)
1/4 inch (6.35 mm)	1/16 inch (1.6 mm)	1/8 inch (3.175 mm)
1/2 inch (12.7 mm)	1/8 inch (3.175 mm)	3/16 inch (4.7625 mm)
1 inch (25.4 mm)	3/16 inch (4.7625 mm)	3/8 inch (9.525 mm)
2 inches (50.8 mm)	3/8 inch (9.525 mm)	3/4 inch (19.05 mm)

This table provides a general guideline. The thickness you choose might vary based on specific needs, such as the tree's species, the branch's actual strength, and your personal experience with how the tree responds to wiring. Always monitor the tree's reaction to wiring and adjust to prevent damage.

FAQ:

What are some common types of wire used for Bonsai tree wiring?

When it comes to wiring bonsai trees, choosing the right type of wire is crucial for effective shaping while ensuring the tree isn't harmed in the process. There are two common types of wire used in bonsai:

Anodized Aluminum Wire:

- Lightweight and flexible, making it easy to manipulate.

- Ideal for beginners due to its ease of use.

- Soft enough to bend without tools for smaller branches.

- Comes in various thicknesses to accommodate different branch sizes.

- The dark color can blend well with most bonsai trees' bark.

Annealed Copper Wire:

- More rigid and provides stronger support for heavier or thicker branches.

- Typically used by more experienced practitioners who require a stronger hold for more defined shaping.

- Must be annealed (heated and cooled) to be flexible enough to wrap around branches.

- Once in place, it holds form strongly and can handle significant weight.

- Copper wire's appearance will change over time as it oxidizes, which can be aesthetically pleasing on certain trees.

Each type of wire has its specific applications and is chosen based on the particular needs of the bonsai and the preference and experience level of the grower. Using the right wire allows for precise control of the tree's shape while minimizing the risk of damage to the bark or branches.

Wiring the trunk

Wiring the trunk of your bonsai is a method used to guide its growth and shape it to your desired style. Here's a step-by-step tutorial on how to wire the trunk effectively:

Step 1: Choose the Right Wire. Select a wire approximately one-third to one-half the trunk's diameter at its base. Copper wire provides more strength and support, whereas aluminum wire is easier to bend. You may need a heavier gauge wire for a thicker trunk or if you intend to make more drastic bends.

Step 2: Anchor the Wire. Take one end of your selected wire and anchor it into the soil. Push it deep enough to hold firm, but be careful not to disrupt the tree's nebari (visible surface roots) or damage the roots below the surface. Position the wire as close to the trunk as possible to ensure solid support for subsequent winding.

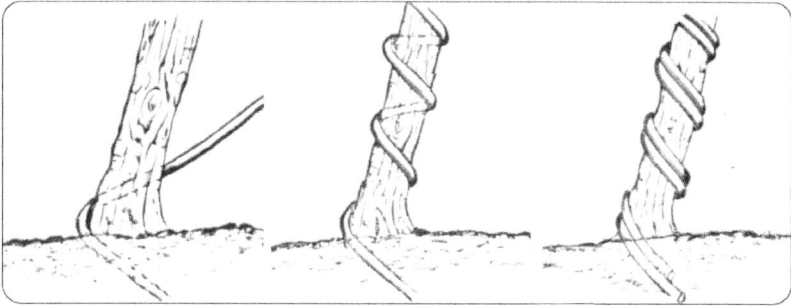

Picture 21: Wiring the Trunk

Step 3: Wrap the Wire Around the Trunk. Gently but firmly wrap the wire around the base of the trunk. The wire should be snug against the trunk, without any gaps. Ensure the wire does not cross over itself and conform to the trunk's natural curves and contours. The contact should be consistent to prevent any damage and allow even distribution of the bending force.

Step 4: Spiral Up the Trunk. Continue wrapping the wire in a spiral pattern up the trunk, maintaining even spacing between the coils. The recommended angle for wrapping is usually between 45° to 55° relative to the trunk. This angle provides a good balance between holding power and flexibility, allowing the trunk to thicken without growing over the wire too quickly.

Step 5: Use a Second Wire for Strength (if necessary). If you plan to make a significant bend, reinforcing the trunk with a second piece of wire might be necessary. This is particularly true for coniferous trees, which can be more resistant to bending. When adding a second wire, run it parallel to the first, keeping the wires next to each other and twisting them together gently as you move up the trunk. The goal is to double the strength without doubling the pressure on any one part of the trunk.

The wiring process is both an art and a science. Patience and practice are key, as is regular observation of the tree to ensure it is responding well to the wire without being damaged. The tree will dictate how it best bends and shapes, so listen to it, and let it guide you.

FAQ:

How long should the wire be left on the branches before removing it?

The length of time you should leave wire on bonsai branches depends on several factors, including the species of tree, the rate of growth, the thickness of the branch, the time of year, and the climate.

There isn't a one-size-fits-all answer, but here are some general guidelines to consider: For fast-growing species, especially during their active growing season, the wire might need to be removed or adjusted after a few months to prevent it from cutting into the expanding bark. For slower-growing species or when wiring during a dormant period, the wire may need to be in place for a year or sometimes even longer.

Young, vigorous trees tend to thicken more quickly than mature, slower-growing trees, which means the wire on younger trees may need to be removed sooner. The size of the branch is also significant; thinner branches will take shape faster than thicker ones and therefore, the wire can be removed earlier.

To avoid damage, it's crucial to check the wired branches regularly for signs that the wire is beginning to bite into the bark. Remove the wire from the top part of the branch and lightly touch it. If it doesn't shift into a different shape, it means the form is completed and the wire can be removed.

It's important to remove wiring before it cuts into the bark and leaves a scar, as these marks can be permanent and detract from the aesthetic of the bonsai. But keep in mind, removing the wire too early can mean the branch hasn't 'set' in its new position and may spring back, so monitoring and judgment are key.

Common wiring problems

Common wiring problems can occur when you're shaping your Bonsai, especially if you're new to the technique. Here are some frequent issues to be aware of and how to avoid or fix them:

Wire Cutting into Bark: This happens if the wire is left on for too long, the tree is growing rapidly, or the wire was applied too tightly. To prevent this, check your wires regularly and remove them before they start to dig into the bark.

Incorrect Wire Size: Using wire that is too thick can damage the tree, while wire that is too thin won't hold the branch in place. You need to choose the right size of wire for each branch, generally one-third the diameter of the branch.

Over-wiring: Applying too much wire to a branch can restrict growth or even cause it to die back. Use only as much wire as you need to shape the branch.

Improper Wiring Technique: The wire should be wrapped at an angle of 45 degrees to the branch and with even spacing between the coils. Wires that cross over each other or are wrapped too loosely/ tightly can harm the tree and be ineffective.

Bending Branches Too Far: If a branch is bent too sharply or too quickly, it can snap. Gradually shape branches and use guy wires for heavy bending.

Neglecting the Tree After Wiring: It's important to continue regular care, including watering, fertilizing, and checking for pests. Neglect can hinder the tree's recovery from the stress of wiring.

Failing to Adjust Wires: As branches grow, the tension in the wire changes. Periodic adjustments might be necessary so that the branch can set in its new shape without getting damaged.

Removing Wire Precipitously: When unwiring, do it carefully. Cut the wires rather than unwinding them, which can damage the bark or disturb the new shape of the branch.

By being aware of these common problems and monitoring your Bonsai closely, you can enjoy the benefits of shaping your tree without causing it undue stress or injury.

FAQ:

How can I prevent wires from cutting into the bark of my Bonsai tree?

Preventing wire from cutting into the bark of your bonsai tree is an important part of the wiring process.

Here are some tips to keep your tree healthy while it's wired:

Choose the Correct Wire Size: Using the appropriate wire diameter for the branch you're shaping is crucial. A wire that's too thin won't hold the branch effectively, and you may over-tighten it, leading to damage. Conversely, a wire that's too thick can be overly rigid and cause unnecessary pressure on the branch.

Apply Wire Properly: When wiring, ensure that the wire is wrapped snugly but not too tight. The coils should be close enough to support the branch when bent but not so tight that they dig into the bark.

Monitor Growth: Check the wired branches regularly, especially during the growing season, as this is when the tree is expanding most rapidly. Signs like bark beginning to grow over the wire indicate it's time to remove or adjust the wiring.

Time Your Wiring: Try to wire when the tree is not in an active growth phase—usually in the late fall or winter for many species. This can prevent the wire from biting into the fast-growing bark.

Use Protective Materials: On trees with particularly delicate bark, you can use raffia or paper strips underneath the wire to add a protective layer. Soak raffia in water until it becomes pliable, then wrap it around the branch before wiring. This can help distribute the wire pressure more evenly and protect the bark.

Avoid Over-Bending: Gradually shape branches with subtle bends. Sharp bends can damage both the wire and the bark and increase the risk of the wire cutting in.

Timely Removal: Remove the wire before it has a chance to cut into the growing branch. Typically, this should be done within several months, but it really depends on the growth rate of your tree.

Careful Removal: Use proper wire cutters, and rather than unwinding, which can damage the now-set branches, cut the wire at each turn for a safe removal.

Re-Wiring if Necessary: If the branch hasn't yet set into shape and the wire is beginning to imbed into the bark, you may need to remove and reapply a larger size wire to account for the increased girth of the branch.

By following these steps, you can properly shape your bonsai tree without causing damage to the bark, ensuring your tree remains healthy and beautiful for years to come.

Tips and troubleshooting with wiring

Wiring can be a bit of a challenge when you're just starting out with Bonsai. To help you along, here are some tips and troubleshooting strategies to make sure you wire effectively and keep your tree healthy:

Tips for Wiring:

Always Wire When Branches Are Flexible: Early spring or after a thorough watering can be the best times. This is when the branches are most pliable and least likely to snap.

Use Appropriate Tools: Good-quality wire cutters and Bonsai pliers make a big difference. They should be sharp and properly sized for the gauge of wire you're using.

Start with Thicker Branches: Practice on the thicker, lower branches first. They're typically more robust and can be a little more forgiving as you learn the right tension.

Less Is More: Don't overdo it. Use the minimum amount of wire needed to achieve the desired change in direction or shape.

Consistency: Maintain consistent spacing and tension as you wrap the wire around the branches at a 45-degree angle.

Troubleshooting with Wiring:

Branches Not Holding Shape: If a branch springs back after you wire and shape it, your wire might be too thin. Reapply with a thicker wire, or add a secondary wire alongside the first for more strength.

Wire Scarring: If you see the wire beginning to bite into the bark, it's time to remove it. Next time, monitor the tree more closely and consider whether you're wrapping the wire too tightly.

Wilted Leaves After Wiring: This could indicate the wire is too tight, the branch was damaged during bending, or the tree is stressed and needs water.

Branch Breaks When Wiring: If this happens, don't panic; clean the break and seal it with cut paste if necessary. You can also use splints to support the broken branch until it heals.

Wires Overlap: This can girdle and restrict the flow of nutrients. If you notice overlapping wires, gently reposition them to eliminate crossing.

Keep in mind that every Bonsai species and even individual trees will behave differently. Pay attention to your Bonsai's response to wiring, adapt your technique as needed, and always prioritize the health and well-being of your tree. With practice and patience, wiring will become second nature.

CHAPTER 14

Pruning the tree

P runing is the cornerstone of bonsai aesthetics and health, a way to direct the energy and growth of the tree towards realizing our vision. I'll show you how carefully. This practice requires thoughtfulness. After reading this chapter, you will gain the knowledge you need to make purposeful decisions. And your Bonsai will become healthier and more beautiful.

Initial pruning

Initial pruning is a critical stage in developing your Bonsai as it shapes the future direction of your tree. It can seem daunting, but with a few guiding principles, you can approach this task with confidence. Here's a beginner-friendly look at initial pruning:

Understand the Goal: Your first pruning session is about establishing the fundamental shape and structure. You're setting the stage for how your Bonsai will look for years to come.

Identify Primary Branches: Look at your tree's natural growth and decide which branches will form the primary lines of your design. These are often lower branches that extend outward, providing balance.

Reduce Crowding: Remove any branches that clutter the tree's appearance, such as those growing straight up or down, crossing over others, or growing too close together.

Consider Proportions: In miniature tree design, proportions matter. Initial pruning helps keep the tree in proportion to its size. It's about creating a sense of age and realism that connects with the viewer.

Use the Right Tools: Sharp, clean pruning shears or concave cutters are essential. They make precise cuts that heal well and minimize scarring.

Step-by-Step Approach: Start by cutting back the most obvious branches that don't fit your desired shape or ones that detract from the tree's balance. Then, gradually refine your tree's form.

Timing: The ideal time for initial pruning is when the tree is healthy and before a growth period, usually in early spring for most species.

Recuperation: After pruning, allow your tree time to recover before undertaking other major activities like repotting.

Don't Over-Prune: A common mistake is to remove too much at once. Remember, it's easier to prune more later than to replace a branch that's been cut.

By taking your time and observing these principles, initial pruning becomes less about cutting away and more about revealing the essence of your Bonsai. It's a process that marries your vision with the inherent beauty of nature.

FAQ:

How do I determine which branches are the primary branches during initial pruning?

Determining the primary branches during initial pruning is a crucial step in creating a pleasing bonsai form. Here's a step-by-step guide to help you identify the primary branches:

Study the Tree's Structure: Take a good look at your bonsai from all angles. Consider the tree's natural lines and flow, as the primary branches should complement the tree's overall shape.

Identify the Trunk Line: The primary branches should emerge from a visually strong and well-established trunk. Look for a good trunk line that will set the foundation for your tree's design.

Consider Branch Placement: Ideally, primary branches should not emerge directly opposite one another, as this can create a 'barbell' effect. They should be staggered and emerge at different heights along the trunk.

Look for Balance: Choose branches that will balance the tree visually. This includes not just side-to-side balance but also front-to-back. The first primary branch, often the lowest on the trunk, usually extends from the front or back and sets the tone for subsequent branches.

Select Healthy Branches: Make sure the branches you're considering as primary branches are healthy and vigorous. Weak or damaged branches may not thrive and therefore aren't good candidates.

Evaluate Branch Thickness: Primary branches should be thicker than the secondary branches and diminish in thickness as they move outward from the trunk, with the thickest branch usually being the first primary branch.

Understand Bonsai Aesthetics: Familiarize yourself with the principles of bonsai aesthetics pertaining to branch selection. For instance, the rule of thirds can be applied to the first primary branch, which should ideally be about one-third of the way up the trunk.

Vision for the Future: Choose branches that have potential for development. Think about how they'll grow over time and contribute to the tree's design.

Remove Unnecessary Branches: After deciding on the primary branches, you may begin to prune unnecessary branches. This could include branches that are growing straight upwards or downwards, are too close together, or are crossing over each other in a way that disrupts the design.

Take Your Time: Don't rush the selection process. It's important to make thoughtful decisions, as removing a branch is irreversible.

Remember, the primary branches are the framework of the bonsai. Their selection and development are fundamental to the aesthetic and health of the tree. If you're ever in doubt, it can be helpful to take a photo of the tree and sketch your intended design, or even consult more experienced bonsai enthusiasts or professionals for their insights.

Choosing the right direction for growth

Choosing the right direction for growth is like charting a course for a journey; it dictates the future shape and character of your Bonsai. Here's how to set your tree on the right path:

Observation: Begin by studying the natural growth pattern of your tree. Notice how the branches and trunk naturally curve or extend. This will give you insight into the most harmonious direction for growth.

Design Intent: Consider the style you're aiming for. Whether it's formal upright, slanting, or cascade, your choice of growth direction should support this final vision.

Balance and Proportion: A well-designed Bonsai is balanced. This doesn't necessarily mean symmetrical but balanced in a way that the tree doesn't look like it's leaning heavily to one side or the other unless that's part of your intended style.

Branch Selection: Choose branches that contribute to your design and encourage them to grow by careful positioning, pruning, and wiring. Remove or redirect those that conflict with your tree's direction of growth.

Apical Dominance: Understand that trees have a tendency to grow stronger at the top and outer edges, known as apical dominance. Sometimes you'll need to trim back the dominant part to encourage lower and inner branches.

Future Growth: When choosing a direction, think several steps ahead. How will the branches you encourage now impact the tree's shape in the future?

Tree's Vigor: Strong, healthy trees can be encouraged to grow in more directions, while weaker trees may need a more conservative approach.

Environmental Considerations: Ensure your tree's direction of growth doesn't expose it to issues like constant strong winds or insufficient light which could stunt its development.

Remember, directing growth is a gradual process that requires patience and periodic reassessment. Each decision you make affects the tree's future. Approach this responsibility with care and respect for the tree's natural tendencies, and you'll be rewarded with a dynamic and harmonious Bonsai.

FAQ:

How can I determine the natural growth pattern of my Bonsai tree?

Determining the natural growth pattern of your bonsai tree is essential for enabling its most authentic and aesthetically pleasing presentation.

Here's how you can ascertain the innate character of your bonsai:

Watch how your tree grows throughout the seasons. Notice which direction the branches and leaves naturally tend to reach towards, and where the strongest growth occurs. Different species have different typical growth patterns. Research the natural habit of your bonsai's species in the wild to understand how it might want to grow in a constrained environment.

Often the trunk will lean or angle in a certain direction, indicating the tree's natural inclination. Is it growing straight up, slanting to one side, or perhaps twisting? The angles at which branches grow from the trunk can tell you a lot about a tree's natural tendencies. Some trees have upward-reaching branches, while others may droop or extend horizontally.

The visible surface roots (nebari) can provide clues to the tree's growth pattern. Balanced and radial nebari suggest stability, while uneven nebari might indicate a tree that's adapted to grow on uneven terrain, like a rocky cliff face. The way the leaves orient themselves in relation to the sun—phototropism—can give you insights into the optimal front for display and how the tree might fill out with foliage over the seasons. To work with the natural growth pattern of your bonsai, it's important to provide conditions conducive to its well-being: adequate sunlight, proper watering, and nutrition.

When wiring and shaping, always consider and respect the tree's innate growth tendencies. By aligning your care and styling with the tree's natural growth pattern, you allow the bonsai to flourish while enhancing its inherent beauty.

Selecting the branch to prune

Selecting the branch to prune is a critical decision in the art of Bonsai. Here's a look at how to choose the right branches:

Structural Soundness: Start by examining the tree's structure. You're looking for a good balance, where branches aren't cluttering the tree or crossing over one another in a way that disrupts the design.

Branch Health: Check for any signs of damage or disease. Prune away unhealthy branches to prevent the spread of disease and to redistribute the tree's energy to healthier parts.

Growth Direction: Observe the direction in which the branches grow. Prune those that grow inward towards the center of the tree or straight up and down, as they break the natural flow.

Thickness and Spacing: Remove branches that are too thick compared to the rest, as these can look out of scale. Also ensure there's adequate space between branches to allow for light and air circulation.

Taper and Transition: A natural-looking Bonsai will have a trunk and branches that taper smoothly. Prune away branches that disrupt this gradual transition in thickness.

Taking the time to choose the right branches for pruning helps to ensure the beauty and health of your Bonsai. Every cut is an irreversible decision; therefore, pruning should be approached meditatively, respecting the existing beauty of the tree while guiding it towards an improved future form.

When and how much to prune?

Timing and amount are vital factors when it comes to pruning your Bonsai. Here's a beginner-friendly guide on when to prune and how much should be cut:

When to Prune:

Seasonal Timing: Many trees respond best to pruning in late winter or early spring before the growth surge. However, maintenance pruning can be done throughout the growing season for certain species.

After Flowering: If your Bonsai blooms, wait to prune until right after the flowering period is over to avoid cutting off buds.

Tree Health: Only prune when your tree is healthy. Pruning can be stressful, so you want to ensure it's at its strongest to recover.

Observation: Look for indicators, such as buds beginning to swell, as signs that it's a good time to prune.

How Much to Prune:

Conservative Approach: For beginners, it's often wise to prune conservatively. Leave room for error and for the tree to recover.

Rule of Thirds: A good rule of thumb is to never remove more than one-third of a tree's foliage at once. This helps maintain sufficient leaves for photosynthesis and encourages new growth.

One Step at a Time: Prune gradually, especially when shaping. Evaluate the effect of each cut before proceeding. You can always prune more later, but you can't put a branch back once it's cut.

Shaping vs. Maintenance: Understand the difference between structural pruning for shape (which is more drastic) and maintenance pruning (which is a bit lighter) to encourage dense growth and small leaves.

Balancing Light and Energy: Remove enough foliage to allow light to reach the inner and lower parts of the tree, promoting growth throughout.

Future Planning: Prune with the future in mind. The shape you desire next year starts with pruning decisions made today.

By respecting these guidelines, you'll ensure your Bonsai remains not just alive but thriving, full of potential for years of continuing development. Remember, patience and observation are key components of successful pruning.

Different pruning technique

Pruning is not a one-size-fits-all approach. Different techniques are used to achieve various effects and to maintain the health and appearance of your Bonsai. Here's a rundown of various pruning techniques for beginners:

Maintenance Pruning: This is done to maintain the shape of the Bonsai by periodically trimming back new growth. Use sharp scissors to cut back to two or three leaves on each shoot.

Structural Pruning: This is typically done during the dormant season. It involves making significant cuts to shape the primary structure of the tree, which includes choosing the main branches and establishing the trunk line.

Pinching: This is a more delicate technique used mainly on softer or juvenile growth, particularly with conifers. It involves pinching out the new growth tips to encourage back-budding and to maintain compact growth.

Defoliation: Applied mostly to deciduous trees, this advanced technique involves removing leaves during the growing season to encourage a second flush of smaller leaves and to improve light penetration and air circulation.

Leaf Pruning: This is often used on deciduous trees to reduce leaf size. Leaves are parti-pruned by cutting away large leaves or reducing them in size, allowing light into the interior of the canopy to stimulate bud production.

Root Pruning: When repotting, it is sometimes necessary to prune the roots to encourage new feeder roots and to fit the tree back into its pot. This should be done with care, knowing that significant root pruning can be stressful for the tree.

Each technique requires a measure of knowledge and control, and a deep understanding of how your particular Bonsai species responds to pruning. Before beginning, always sanitize your tools to prevent the spread of disease. Take your time with each cut, considering the long-term effects on your tree's health and design. With experience, you'll learn which techniques to use to bring out the best in your Bonsai.

Tools for pruning

Having the right tools for pruning can make all the difference, not just to the immediate appearance of your Bonsai, but also to its long-term health and development. Here's a beginner's guide to the essential tools you'll need for pruning Bonsai trees:

Bonsai Scissors: These are the most frequently used tools for pruning leaves and fine, small branches. They have a very sharp blade and a large handle, designed for precision cutting and ease of use.

Concave Branch Cutters: These specialized tools are designed to make a clean, concave cut that heals with the least visible scarring on the tree. They are perfect for removing larger branches.

Knob Cutters: Similar to concave branch cutters but with a more rounded edge, knob cutters are used to cut deeper into the trunk or branches to remove unsightly knobs or stumps.

Wire Cutters: When you're wiring your tree for training, you'll also need wire cutters to remove the wire without damaging the branches.

Jin Pliers: These are used for creating jin and shari, the seasoned deadwood effects on Bonsai. They can also be used for removing small branches and peeling bark.

Folding Pruning Saw: For significant cuts on larger branches or trunks, a small pruning saw is needed. It should be sharp and precise to ensure clean cuts.

Pruning Paste or Sealer: After cutting a branch, it's important to apply pruning paste or sealer to protect the wound and facilitate healing.

Tips for Choosing and Using Pruning Tools:

Quality Matters: Invest in high-quality tools made specifically for Bonsai to ensure clean cuts that heal well and last longer.

Keep Them Clean: Clean your tools after each use to prevent the spread of disease between your trees. Sterilize them if you've been working on a sick tree.

Keep Them Sharp: Dull blades can damage branches and create rough cuts that take longer to heal.

Understand Their Use: Each tool has a specific purpose; understand what each one does and use it only for its intended task.

With these tools in your kit, you'll be well-prepared to maintain your Bonsai's shape and health. Remember, good tools are an investment in your Bonsai's future.

CHAPTER 15

Root pruning

Root pruning should typically be done every two to three years for most Bonsai trees. However, the frequency can vary depending on the species, age, and growth rate of the tree, as well as the size of the pot.

Young, Fast-Growing Trees: May need root pruning more frequently, sometimes annually, to ensure they don't become pot-bound and to encourage a dense, fibrous root system.

Older, Slow-Growing Trees: These often require less frequent root pruning, perhaps every three to five years, due to their slower growth rate.

Pot Size: Trees in smaller pots may require more frequent root pruning to maintain the balance between the root mass and the pot's confining space.

Always monitor the health of your Bonsai to determine the best timing for root pruning, and adjust your schedule according to how quickly the tree's roots fill the pot. It's also worth noting that root pruning should be avoided during the tree's dormancy period and should ideally be done in the early spring to give the tree a full growing season to recover.

CHAPTER 16

Seasonal tasks

A s the wheel of the year turns, so too does the cycle of care for your Bonsai tree. Each season brings with it a unique set of tasks designed to harmonize with the natural rhythms of your miniature masterpiece. In the chapter on "Seasonal Tasks", we will guide you through the specific care requirements that spring, summer, autumn, and winter command.

Spring tasks

Spring is a bustling season for Bonsai enthusiasts, as your trees emerge from their winter dormancy with a burst of energy. Here's what you need to focus on during this time of renewal:

Repotting: Early spring is the prime time for repotting as the tree's roots begin to grow. It's the moment to change the soil, prune the roots, and possibly upgrade to a larger pot if needed. Not every tree requires annual repotting; it depends on the age and species of the tree.

Feeding: With new growth on the horizon, your Bonsai will be hungry for nutrients. Begin your regular feeding program as soon as you see new growth, using a balanced fertilizer to support healthy development.

Pruning: Prune any unwanted branches in early spring. This is also the time to trim back last year's growth to shape the Bonsai and encourage a denser canopy. Be mindful of flowering Bonsai species; pruning should be done after they bloom.

Wiring: If you need to wire branches to train them into new positions, spring is a good time to do so as the tree's flexibility increases. However, keep a close eye on the wires to ensure they don't cut into the rapidly growing bark.

Watering: As temperatures rise and daylight hours increase, your watering routine will need to be adjusted. Monitor soil moisture carefully, as the tree will consume more water than it did in the cooler months.

Spring tasks set the pace for the rest of the year, thus paying close attention to your Bonsai's needs during this season is paramount. Each of these tasks plays a role in the health, growth, and aesthetic of your Bonsai, setting it on the right path to flourish for the rest of the year.

Summer tasks

Summer brings a wave of growth and activity to the Bonsai world. It can be a challenging time, as the heat and increased sunlight impact the care routine. Here's what you need to focus on:

Watering: This is critical as the warmer weather and longer days can dry out the soil much faster. You may need to water your Bonsai once a day or even twice during heat waves. Always check the soil moisture level to gauge the need for watering.

Pest and Disease Control: With the rise in temperature and humidity, pests and diseases become more active. Keep a watchful eye for signs of infestation or illness, such as discoloration, spots on leaves, or sudden leaf drop. Promptly address any issues with appropriate and safe treatments.

Fertilizing: Continue feeding your Bonsai with appropriate fertilizers to support vigorous growth, but be careful not to overfeed. Pay attention to the specific needs of your tree species, as requirements can vary.

Pruning: Summer is often the time for maintenance pruning to manage the new growth and maintain your tree's shape. Regular trimming will also encourage a denser canopy and keep the tree size in check.

Shade and Ventilation: Protect your Bonsai from the scorching midday sun, especially if you live in an area with intensely hot summers. Providing shade during the hottest parts of the day can prevent leaf burn. Good airflow helps prevent fungal diseases, which can be problematic in high humidity.

By managing these tasks diligently, you can ensure your Bonsai remains healthy and vigorous throughout the hot summer months.

Autumn tasks

As autumn rolls in, it marks a time of preparation and transition for your Bonsai trees. This season's tasks are centered around readying them for the colder months ahead while capitalizing on the fall growth spurt. Here's what to attend to:

Watering Adjustment: As the days shorten and temperatures drop, your Bonsai will require less water. Keep a close eye on the soil moisture and adjust your watering schedule accordingly to avoid waterlogged soil, which can lead to root rot.

Fertilizing: It's time to switch to a low-nitrogen, high-phosphorus fertilizer to encourage root development and help strengthen the tree for the winter. Fertilize less frequently as the tree's growth slows down.

Structural Pruning: Autumn is ideal for major pruning tasks. Since the foliage is less dense, you can easily assess the tree's structure and make decisions about branch removal and future growth.

Pest & Disease Prevention: Continue monitoring for pests and diseases. Clear any fallen leaves or debris around the Bonsai pot to reduce the risk of mold and fungal infections.

Preparing for Winter: Depending on your climate, begin preparations for wintering your Bonsai. This might involve gradually reducing the amount of daylight they receive and moving them to a sheltered location.

Enjoy Autumnal Changes: For deciduous species, this is a time to appreciate the seasonal color changes they offer. Make sure they are positioned to enjoy their display safely without harsh elements which could damage the tree.

By addressing these autumn tasks, you'll not only fortify your Bonsai for winter but also enhance their health and beauty for the following spring.

Winter tasks

Winter, a time when many Bonsai trees go into dormancy, is less demanding in terms of routine care tasks. However, this quiet period still requires vigilant attention to keep your Bonsai healthy and ready for spring. These are the winter tasks you should focus on:

Protection: If your climate experiences freezing temperatures, you'll need to protect your Bonsai. Options include placing them in a cold frame, unheated garage, or burying the pot in the ground. The goal is to keep the roots from freezing, which can damage or kill the tree.

Watering: Although the trees' water requirements decrease in winter, they still need some hydration. Again, respond to the tree's needs rather than maintaining a strict watering schedule.

Winter Pruning: For non-deciduous trees, winter can be an ideal time for structural pruning because the tree is dormant. However, this does not apply to all species, so make sure to research your specific Bonsai type.

Planning the Year Ahead: Use this slower season to evaluate your Bonsai's progress over the past year and plan for the year ahead. Think about what worked well, what you'd like to change, and any new techniques you'd like to try.

Checking for Pests and Diseases: While less common in winter, it's still necessary to check your tree regularly for any signs of pests or disease.

Maintaining the health of your Bonsai tree during winter requires careful attention to temperature and moisture levels but can be less intensive than other seasons. Winter is a time of rest for many trees, preparing them for the vigor of spring.

Occasional tasks

I n the world of Bonsai, certain tasks don't adhere to a strict schedule but are essential for the health and presentation of your prized tree. The chapter "Occasional Tasks" will guide you through these intermittent but crucial duties. Read this chapter to fine-tune your Bonsai care practices and ensure the longevity and beauty of your miniature trees.

Unwiring

Unwiring is an occasional but important task in Bonsai care, as leaving wire on for too long can damage the tree. As your Bonsai grows, the branches will thicken, and the wires can cut into the bark, potentially harming or even killing the branch if not removed in time.

Here are some tips for unwiring your Bonsai:

Timing: Monitor your Bonsai's growth closely and begin unwiring when you see signs that the wire is starting to dig into the bark but before it causes deep scars.

Careful Removal: When unwiring, be gentle. Use wire cutters to snip the wire at each turn rather than unwinding it, which can damage the branches.

Branch Stability: After the wire is removed, check if the branch remains in place. Some branches may require re-wiring if they haven't fully set in their desired shape.

Healing Time: Give your Bonsai time to heal after unwiring before performing other stressful tasks such as heavy pruning or repotting.

Inspect for Damage: If any branches have been scarred by the wire, evaluate the extent of the damage. Light scarring can be a normal part of the styling process and might add character to the Bonsai, but severe girdling marks may warrant restorative care or could serve as a learning experience for future wiring.

By unwiring carefully and at the right time, you'll ensure your Bonsai tree continues to grow as desired without the drawback of wire marks or damaged branches.

Sterilize tools

Sterilizing your Bonsai tools is an essential practice that prevents the spread of disease and pests from one tree to another. It's an occasional task that should be done regularly, especially after working on a tree that is sick or you suspect might be diseased.

Here's how you can sterilize your Bonsai tools effectively:

Rubbing Alcohol: Use either isopropyl alcohol (at least 70%) or ethanol. Soak the blades of the tools for a couple of minutes, then wipe them clean with a cloth. Alcohol evaporates quickly, allowing you to use the tools soon after sterilization.

Bleach Solution: Create a solution of 1 part household bleach to 9 parts water. Soak the tools for about 30 minutes, then rinse them with water and dry them thoroughly to prevent rusting. Use gloves to protect your hands from the bleach.

Heat: For metal tools, you can also use heat to sterilize them. This can be done by passing the tool through a flame until the metal is hot, but this method requires caution to avoid weakening the metal or burning yourself.

Commercial Solutions: There are commercial sterilizing solutions and sprays available specifically designed for garden tools that can be used following the manufacturer's instructions.

Regardless of the method, ensure that the tools are completely dry before storing to prevent rust, and always handle sharp tools with care. Ensuring your tools are clean not only promotes the health of your Bonsai trees but also maintains the integrity of the tools themselves.

Tread deadwood

Treating deadwood on a Bonsai, known as "jin" and "shari," involves creating and preserving areas on the Bonsai that mimic the natural aging and weathering effects found in old trees in the wild. This technique can enhance the tree's character and aesthetic value.

Here's how to go about it:

Creation: To create deadwood, carefully strip away the bark and cambium layer on the selected branch or part of the trunk using jin pliers or a sharp knife, exposing the underlying wood.

Shaping: Once exposed, you can shape the deadwood using carving tools to give it a natural and weathered appearance. Be careful not to damage the surrounding living tissue as you work.

Preservation: Deadwood on a Bonsai can be vulnerable to rot and decay, especially in damp environments. To protect it, apply a wood hardener or preservative. Products like lime sulfur are commonly used as they also bleach the wood, giving it a more natural, aged look.

Timing: The best time to treat deadwood is during the tree's growing season when it can heal and compartmentalize any potential damage that may occur during the creation process.

Maintenance: Over time, reapply lime sulfur or another suitable preservative to maintain the deadwood's appearance and health. Additionally, remove any debris or moss that accumulates on the deadwood to prevent moisture retention and decay.

Treating deadwood is an occasional task that adds an intriguing narrative element to your Bonsai, expressing resilience and the passage of time in your living art.

FAQ:

When is the best time to treat deadwood on a Bonsai?

The best time to treat deadwood on a Bonsai is usually during the tree's active growing season, which tends to be in the spring or early summer. This is when the tree is most vigorous and can heal any wounds or stress caused by the process more effectively.

Spring is particularly good because the increased sap flow can help seal and compartmentalize the areas where you remove living tissue to create the deadwood. Plus, with the full growing season ahead, the tree has ample time to recover before winter dormancy.

It's important to avoid creating deadwood during the late fall or winter when the tree is not actively growing as it won't be able to heal as well, leaving it more vulnerable to pests and diseases. Always ensure that the tree is healthy and in a strong growing phase before undertaking any significant work like this.

Protect from high-temperature

Protecting your Bonsai from high temperatures is essential during the hot summer months to ensure it thrives. Bonsai trees can suffer from leaf burn, dehydration, and heat stress if not properly shielded from intense heat.

Here are some steps to keep your Bonsai cool:

Shade: Provide some shade during the hottest parts of the day. This can be done using a shade cloth, moving the Bonsai to a shaded area, or placing it under the canopy of a larger plant.

Watering: Increase the frequency of watering to cool the soil and provide moisture for transpiration. Water early in the morning or in the evening to reduce evaporation.

Positioning: Move the Bonsai to a location that receives morning sunlight but is protected from the more intense afternoon sun.

Air Circulation: Ensure that there is good air circulation around your Bonsai to help dissipate heat, but avoid placing it in areas where hot, dry winds could further stress the plant.

Humidity Trays: Place your Bonsai on humidity trays filled with water and pebbles. This can help increase local humidity and keep the roots cool.

Mulching: Apply a layer of mulch over the soil surface to help retain moisture and keep the roots cool.

Avoid Fertilizing: It's best to avoid fertilizing during very hot periods as this can increase stress on the tree.

By protecting your Bonsai from high temperatures, you help ensure its health and longevity, allowing it to continue being a source of beauty and enjoyment.

Troubleshooting

Troubleshooting is an important aspect of Bonsai care. It involves observing your tree closely, identifying potential issues, and taking corrective actions.

Here are common problems and how to troubleshoot them:

Yellowing Leaves: This could indicate overwatering, underwatering, nutrient deficiencies, or poor soil drainage. Check the soil moisture and adjust your watering schedule. If the soil isn't draining well, it might be time to repot.

Brown or Crispy Leaves: Usually a sign of underwatering or low humidity. Increase watering and consider using a humidity tray. Also, protect your Bonsai from direct hot sunlight.

Leaf Drop: A sudden leaf drop can be due to a drastic change in temperature or lighting conditions. Make changes gradual when moving your Bonsai to a new location, and maintain a stable environment.

Weak Growth: If your Bonsai is not producing robust new growth, it might lack nutrients. Ensure you are following a proper fertilizing schedule that fits the species and season.

Pests: Common pests like spider mites, scale, and aphids can cause damage. Use a magnifying glass to inspect for these pests and treat your Bonsai with the appropriate organic or chemical controls.

Fungal Diseases: If you notice any unusual spots or powdery substances on the leaves, it might be a fungal infection. Improve air circulation, reduce humidity, and use a fungicide as necessary.

Always tailor your troubleshooting approach to the specific needs of your Bonsai species, and remember that prevention is often the best measure against issues. Regular care, observation, and maintenance are key to keeping your Bonsai in top health.

CHAPTER 17

Shaping and Displaying your Bonsai

Shaping and displaying your Bonsai are two sides of the same coin; both are crucial to showcasing the beauty and character of your miniature tree. Here's how beginners can approach shaping and displaying their Bonsai:

Shaping Your Bonsai:

Vision: Start with a clear vision of your desired tree shape. Look at natural trees for inspiration, considering forms that resonate with you and fit your tree's natural tendencies.

Pruning: Use pruning to create and maintain the shape by selectively removing unwanted branches and leaves. Remember, less is often more.

Wiring: Carefully apply wire to branches you want to reposition. Gradually shape them over time and be sure to remove the wire before it cuts into the growing branch.

Patience and Adjustment: Shaping is an ongoing process. As your Bonsai matures, it will require regular adjustments to maintain your vision while respecting the tree's growth.

Displaying Your Bonsai:

Choosing the Right Spot: Display your Bonsai where it complements the space around it. Indoors, place it at eye level in a well-lit area but away from direct sunlight which can scorch the leaves. If displayed outdoors, ensure your tree is protected from harsh weather conditions.

The Pot as a Frame: Just as a picture frame complements a photo, your Bonsai pot should match the style and size of your tree. Traditional Bonsai pots are shallow and unobtrusive, designed to focus attention on the tree.

Rotation: Rotate your Bonsai occasionally to ensure all sides receive equal light and to prevent the tree from growing in one direction.

Accent Plants and Decoration: Consider using accent plants and small rocks to enhance your Bonsai presentation. They should not overpower the tree but complement the overall display.

Cleanliness: Keep the tree, pot, and display area clean and free from debris. A well-kept display reflects the care and attention given to the Bonsai.

Remember, your Bonsai is a living art form, and the way you shape and present it should reflect the effort and creativity you have invested. By paying attention to these shaping and displaying tips, even beginners can create stunning Bonsai presentations that truly celebrate the unique beauty of these miniature trees.

CHAPTER 18

Problems you should know about

C aring for a Bonsai tree is a rewarding experience, but it can come with its set of challenges. Here's a beginner-friendly overview of common Bonsai problems and how to address them:

Yellowing Leaves: This may indicate a watering issue or a lack of nutrients. Adjust your watering schedule and ensure you're using the right fertilizer for your Bonsai type.

Drooping Leaves: If the leaves are limp and lifeless, your Bonsai could be thirsty. Check the soil moisture and water adequately. Also, confirm that the pot allows for proper drainage.

Brown, Crispy Leaves: Overexposure to sunlight or under-watering could cause leaves to become dry and crispy. Provide some shade during the hottest part of the day and monitor the soil moisture levels.

Pests: Spider mites, aphids, and scale can suck the sap from your tree. Isolate the affected Bonsai and treat it with an appropriate pesticide, neem oil, or a gentle soap solution.

Fungal Infections: Signs include powdery mildew or black spots on leaves. Increase air circulation, reduce watering, and remove affected parts; fungicides may be necessary for more severe cases.

Overgrown Roots: If your Bonsai is pot-bound, it may display stunted growth or could be pushed up out of the pot. Repot your

Bonsai during its dormant season and prune the roots as necessary.

Wiring Scars: This occurs when wire is left on too long and begins to cut into the bark. Remove the wire carefully and avoid wiring the same section too soon to allow time for the bark to heal.

Weak Growth: This can be caused by insufficient light, poor nutrition, or compacted soil. Make sure your Bonsai gets enough light, fertilize appropriately, and consider repotting if the soil seems dense or lacks aeration.

Whenever you encounter these common problems, assess the issue calmly and act deliberately. Always observe first, diagnose accurately, and then proceed with the solution. Bonsai care is as much about prevention as it is about cure, so regular monitoring and maintenance are key. With vigilance and patience, most Bonsai problems can be resolved, allowing your tree to flourish.

CHAPTER 19

Leading causes of plant death

Frequent watering

Bonsai trees, like all plants, need water to survive. However, there is a delicate balance to be struck. One of the most common causes of Bonsai plant death is over-watering or 'frequent watering.' This subchapter tackles the potential dangers of loving your plant a bit too liberally with water and how to avoid them.

Over-watering your Bonsai can lead to root rot, a condition where the roots of the plant begin to decay in overly moist soil conditions. The roots, lacking oxygen and besieged by fungal growth, fail to function properly which can lead to the plant's demise.

Signs of Over-watering:

- A foul odor emanating from the soil can indicate rotting roots.

- Leaves turning yellow and falling off out of season.

- Stagnant water at the bottom of the pot.

- Pests and fungal gnats are attracted to excessively moist environments.

Preventive Measures:

- Check the soil before watering. Only water when the top layer of soil is dry to the touch.

- Ensure your Bonsai pot has adequate drainage holes to let excess water escape.

- Use well-draining soil that can retain moisture without becoming waterlogged.

- Monitor your Bonsai's watering needs, which can change with the seasons, temperature, and humidity levels.

Fixing the Problem:

- If you detect signs of over-watering, reduce your watering schedule immediately.

- If root rot is suspected, remove the tree from its pot, trim away any blackened or mushy roots, repot with fresh, dry soil, and adjust your watering habits.

Through thoughtful observation and adjustment, you can steer clear of the perils of frequent watering and foster a healthy, flourishing Bonsai.

Rare watering

On the opposite end of the spectrum from frequent watering lies the equally treacherous practice of rare or infrequent watering. Bonsai trees are subjected to the limitations of their small containers, which means careful attention must be paid to their hydration needs.

A Bonsai tree that doesn't receive enough water will show signs of stress. The soil will be dry and hard, leaves will wilt or curl, and the foliage may start to turn yellow or brown and become crisp to the touch. Prolonged dryness can cause the branches and leaves to dry out completely, and the root system can become damaged.

Preventing rare watering is about understanding your Bonsai's specific needs which vary depending on the type of tree, the time of year, and the environment. A diligent watering routine is crucial.

Consequences of Insufficient Watering:

- Stunted growth due to the tree not receiving the necessary nutrients from the soil.

- Leaves and branches dying back as the tree conserves remaining moisture for vital functions.

- Permanent damage to the root system if left unchecked, which can lead to the Bonsai's death.

Correcting Watering Practices:

- Check the topsoil daily, and when the top layer feels dry, it's time to water.

- When watering, do so thoroughly until water runs out of the drainage holes, ensuring the roots are fully saturated.

- Consider investing in a moisture meter to take the guesswork out of watering, especially helpful for beginners.

Remember, consistent care and mindfulness of the Bonsai's environment will help you keep on top of watering requirements, allowing your miniature tree to thrive in its limited space.

Fungus and disasters

Fungus and unexpected disasters present unique challenges in Bonsai care, often resulting in distress or even death of the tree. This subchapter explores how fungal infections and accidental events can impact your Bonsai and offers advice on how to protect against and respond to these threats.

Battling Fungal Invasions: Fungal infections often find their way into a Bonsai through overwatering, inadequate air circulation, or contaminated soil or tools.

Telltale signs include:

- White, powdery mildew on leaves or stems.

- Black spots or patches on foliage indicating a possible black spot fungus.

- Mushrooms or other fungal growths in the soil, which may signify root rot.

Disasters: Disasters can be both natural (such as storms, extreme temperatures, or pests) and man-made (like chemical burns from fertilizers or accidental damage). The key to navigating these disasters is preparation and prompt action.

Preventative Measures:

- Isolate new plants to prevent the spread of potential diseases.

- Use sterile tools and pots when working with your Bonsai.

- Maintain good air circulation in the growing environment.

- Apply a protective layer of mulch to shield the soil from extreme elements.

Recovering from Fungus:

- If you notice fungal growth, isolate the affected Bonsai immediately to avoid cross-contamination.

- Prune away any infected parts of the plant.

- Treat the Bonsai with an appropriate fungicide, following the product's instructions.

Recovering from Disasters:

- In the event of a natural disaster, assess the damage and prune any broken or damaged branches.

- Repot the Bonsai if necessary, replacing any soil that has washed away or become compacted.

• Provide a stable environment for the tree to recuperate, avoiding further stressors.

Understanding these potential threats to your Bonsai's well-being equips you to be vigilant in care and swift in corrective action, ensuring that your precious Bonsai can overcome and thrive.

Yellowing of leaves

Yellowing leaves on a Bonsai can be a cause for concern, signaling that something is amiss with your tree. This subchapter aims to dissect the reasons behind this change in foliage color and offers guidance on identifying the cause and rectifying the issue.

Identifying the Symptoms:Yellow leaves can result from various factors, each requiring a different approach. It's critical to accurately diagnose why the leaves are turning yellow to address the problem effectively.

Common Causes of Leaf Yellowing:

Nutritional Deficiency: Lack of essential nutrients, like nitrogen, can lead to yellowing leaves. Regular feeding with a balanced Bonsai fertilizer can correct this.

Watering Issues: Both overwatering and underwatering can cause leaves to yellow. Check the soil's moisture level and adjust your watering routine accordingly.

Poor Drainage: Make sure the Bonsai pot has proper drainage to prevent water from accumulating around the roots, leading to yellow leaves.

Pests or Disease: Infestations or infections can also lead to yellowing. Inspect your tree for signs of bugs or fungus and treat it as needed.

Aging: It's natural for older leaves to turn yellow and drop off as part of the tree's growth cycle. If the yellowing is on the oldest leaves, it may not be cause for concern.

Solving the Yellowing Dilemma:

- Adjust watering habits, ensuring you're neither drowning the roots nor leaving them too dry.

- Enhance feeding with a proper Bonsai fertilizer, especially if a deficiency is suspected.

- Improve soil quality and pot drainage if the yellowing is due to waterlogged conditions.

- Treat any diseases or pest issues promptly with appropriate solutions.

- When the yellowing is part of the tree's natural lifecycle, simply remove the yellow leaves to maintain aesthetics.

By observing these changes and responding to the potential causes with the appropriate actions outlined in this chapter, you can generally expect to see an improvement in your Bonsai's vigor, preserving the lush green palette of its foliage.

Drying of branches and leaves

The drying of branches and leaves in a Bonsai tree often heralds health issues that, if not promptly addressed, can lead to the decline and possible death of your miniature plant. In this subchapter, we'll look at the reasons behind the desiccation and how to nurture your tree back to health.

Symptoms and Diagnosis: Dried and brittle leaves, coupled with lifeless branches, typically indicate that the tree is not receiving adequate moisture or has been damaged. The causes can be environmental, care-related, or biological.

Common Culprits of Drying:

Underwatering: Consistent lack of water can cause the tree to dry out. Roots may not be able to uptake the nutrients and moisture the plant needs.

Overexposure to Sun or Heat: Too much direct sunlight, especially during hot weather, can scorch leaves and dehydrate branches.

Pest Infestation: Certain pests can drain the sap and moisture from leaves and branches, causing them to dry out.

Disease: Some diseases can clog the tree's vascular system, preventing moisture distribution.

Reviving Your Bonsai:

- Confirm that the Bonsai's watering schedule is aligned with its needs. Adjust as needed to ensure consistent soil moisture.

- Provide shade during the hottest part of the day to protect leaves from burning and drying.

- Examine for pests and treat the plant with an appropriate pesticide or natural remedy.

- Diseased trees should be isolated and treated. Remove all affected parts to prevent spread and apply fungicides if a fungal disease is present.

Prevention Strategy:

- Regular checks of soil moisture levels and the tree's overall well-being can prevent drying.

- Creating a favorable microclimate with balanced humidity can protect against harsh conditions.

- Healthy, vigilant care routines deter pests and disease, reducing the risk of dry branches and leaves.

Understanding these signs and taking decisive action can restore your Bonsai to its natural beauty and help prevent future occurrences of dehydration and drying. Remember, consistent care tailored to your specific Bonsai type is key to avoiding the dry spell that threatens these living works of art.

CHAPTER 20

Pests and diseases

I n the nurturing journey of Bonsai, cultivators must be ever-vigilant against the tiny invaders and silent ailments that can compromise their trees' health. This chapter, "Pests and Diseases," serves as a tactical guide to identifying, combating, and preventing the incursions of pests and the onset of disease in your Bonsai.

Rubbing alcohol and water

The mixture of rubbing alcohol and water creates an inexpensive and effective solution for managing certain pests on Bonsai trees. This subchapter will guide you through the use of this simple yet potent concoction in your pest control regimen.

Preparation: Mix a solution of 70% isopropyl rubbing alcohol with 30% water. For added safety, test the solution on a small part of the Bonsai to ensure it doesn't harm the plant.

Application: Use a spray bottle to lightly mist affected areas, targeting pests directly. The alcohol in the mixture works to dehydrate and kill many soft-bodied insects on contact.

Best Practices:

- Apply during cooler parts of the day to avoid leaf burn, as alcohol can increase the foliage's sensitivity to sunlight.

- Ensure good ventilation if treating your Bonsai indoors to prevent the buildup of alcohol fumes.

- Avoid using the solution on very young or tender foliage, as it may be too harsh.

Post-Treatment Care: After treating your Bonsai with the rubbing alcohol and water mixture, monitor the plant closely for any signs of stress. Rinse the foliage with clean water within a few hours to remove any residual alcohol that can be harmful if left to sit.

With proper use, rubbing alcohol and water can be a practical addition to your pest management toolbox, effectively dealing with outbreaks without the need for harsher chemicals.

Rubbing alcohol and cotton balls

For a precise approach to pest control on Bonsai trees, the use of rubbing alcohol and cotton balls can be particularly effective. This subchapter will explain how to tackle pests on a smaller scale, ensuring your Bonsai remains unharmed in the process.

Technique: Dip a cotton ball in rubbing alcohol (isopropyl alcohol, ideally 70%) and gently apply it to the infected areas of the Bonsai. The targeted application is ideal for spot-treating pests like scale, mites, and aphids without exposing the entire plant to alcohol.

Advantages: This method allows you to control exactly where the alcohol goes, reducing the risk of damage to the leaves and stems of delicate Bonsai trees. It's especially suited for treating areas where pests congregate, such as under leaves or in nooks of the branches.

Procedure:

- Sparsely dab the pests with the alcohol-soaked cotton ball.

- Work systematically to ensure all infected areas are treated.

- Avoid over-saturation, as excess alcohol can harm the Bonsai's foliage and bark.

Safety Measures:

- Use gloves to protect your hands from prolonged alcohol exposure.

- Perform the treatment in a well-ventilated area to avoid inhaling fumes.

- Consider the Bonsai species' sensitivity before applying alcohol.

Post Application: After using alcohol, keep an eye on the treated spots over the following days to ensure the pests do not return and that the Bonsai shows no adverse reaction to the treatment. If necessary, repeat the process in about a week to deal with any lingering or newly hatched pests.

This precise method, when followed with care, offers a straightforward and effective way to address pest issues, helping keep your Bonsai healthy and beautiful.

Neem oil using

Neem oil, derived from the neem tree, is a natural pesticide that's favored in the Bonsai community for its effectiveness and safety. This subchapter will navigate through the usage of neem oil as a means to protect your Bonsai from a host of common pests.

Benefits of Neem Oil: Neem oil works as a repellent, antifeedant, and egg-laying deterrent for many insects, making it an all-in-one solution for pest control. It's organic and biodegradable, posing less risk to beneficial insects when used correctly.

Preparing the Solution: Most neem oil products come concentrated and need to be diluted before application. Mix the oil with water as directed on the product label, often with a few drops of mild liquid soap to help emulsify the oil.

Application Process: Apply the neem oil solution as a foliar spray, coating the leaves, branches, and soil. The oil works best if applied late in the day or on cloudy days to avoid leaf burn and to ensure maximum coverage when pests are most active.

Frequency of Use: For active infestations, apply neem oil every 7 to 14 days until the pests are under control. As a preventative measure, a monthly application during the growing season can help deter new infestations.

Considerations:

- Test the solution on a small area first to ensure it doesn't cause a reaction on the Bonsai.

- Don't use neem oil on very young plants or during extreme temperatures.

- Shake the mixture regularly during application to keep the oil and water combined.

Following these guidelines will make "Neem Oil Using" an essential and natural part of your Bonsai plant care, keeping pests in check while maintaining the overall health and beauty of your Bonsai.

Pesticides

The intentional application of pesticides can be a powerful defensive line against the onslaught of pests that threaten our beloved Bonsai trees. In this subchapter, we will discuss the prudent use of these chemical agents and spotlight some popular brands available in the USA market.

Understanding Pesticides: Pesticides are substances designed to prevent, destroy, repel, or mitigate any pest. They come in different formulations, including sprays, granules, and systemic varieties, each designed for specific problems and plant types.

Choosing a Pesticide: Select a pesticide based on the specific pests you're dealing with and the Bonsai species you have. Always read the label for application instructions and safety precautions to minimize any risk to the plant and the environment.

Popular Pesticide Brands:

Bonide: Known for a wide array of products suitable for Bonsai care, Bonide offers both organic and traditional options to tackle everything from fungal diseases to insect infestations.

Bayer Advanced: A choice for many Bonsai enthusiasts, Bayer Advanced provides systemic products that protect the tree from the inside out, offering long-term pest control.

Monterey: This brand offers a variety of lawn and garden products, with pesticides that are endorsed by many for their effectiveness on Bonsai pests.

Safer Brand: For those looking for organic solutions, Safer Brand provides options like insecticidal soaps and neem oil that are gentler on plants and the surrounding environment.

Application Tips:

- Apply in the early morning or late afternoon to avoid the heat of the day.

- Avoid windy days to prevent drift and potential harm to non-target areas.

- Follow the manufacturer's guidelines for dosage and frequency to avoid over-application.

Safety Measures:

- Wear protective gloves and eyewear when handling and applying pesticides.

- Store pesticides away from pets and children in a secure location.

- Dispose of any unused pesticide or empty containers properly, according to local regulations.

Aftercare: Following the application of pesticides, monitor the Bonsai for signs of improvement or any adverse reactions. Be prepared to adjust your pest management approach as needed to achieve the best health for your Bonsai.

Employing pesticides requires responsibility and care. Used correctly, they can be an integral part of your Bonsai maintenance routine, offering protection and peace of mind as you cultivate these miniature masterpieces.

Insecticides

Insecticides are a class of pesticides specifically formulated to target and eliminate harmful insect populations that can damage Bonsai trees. This subchapter will guide you through the usage of insecticides and highlight some well-known brands that are widely used by Bonsai enthusiasts across the USA.

Strategic Application: The key to using insecticides effectively is to apply them at the right time and in the correct manner. You must identify the pests afflicting your Bonsai accurately and choose a product that targets those insects without harming your tree.

Popular Insecticide Brands:

Ortho: A household name, Ortho provides a range of insect control products that are potent against a variety of common Bonsai pests.

Spectracide: Offering solutions from general-purpose insect killers to products tailored for specific pests, Spectracide is recognized for its effectiveness and ease of use.

BioAdvanced: Previously known as Bayer Advanced, BioAdvanced insecticides are notable for their systemic action, protecting Bonsai trees from the inside out.

Captain Jack's Deadbug Brew by Bonide: This product contains Spinosad, a natural substance that is effective against many pests and is touted for its eco-friendly profile.

Utilizing Insecticides Safely:

- Carefully read and follow the insecticide label for instructions on mixing, application, and safety precautions.

- Use personal protective equipment, such as gloves and glasses, to avoid direct contact with the chemicals.

- Apply insecticides in calm weather to prevent drift to non-target areas and creatures.

Environmental Consideration:Insecticides can impact beneficial insects and other wildlife. Use them thoughtfully to maintain a balance in the ecosystem. Consider starting with less toxic options, like horticultural oils or insecticidal soaps, before resorting to stronger chemicals.

Ongoing Management: After applying an insecticide, observe your Bonsai closely for effectiveness and any signs of stress or damage. You may need to apply additional treatments to fully control the infestation, depending on the product's instruction and the life cycle of the pest.

Remember that responsible use of insecticides is fundamental to maintaining the harmony and health of your Bonsai. With a judicious approach and careful brand selection, you can safeguard your Bonsai from harmful insects while nurturing the natural beauty it represents.

Pest types and how to prevent

A Bonsai tree can become a host to a variety of pests, each with the potential to weaken or even kill the tree. Understanding the types of pests, their behaviors, and effective preventive measures is key to ensuring the longevity and health of your Bonsai. In this chapter, we will uncover common pests and share useful suggestions for preventing infestations.

Aphids: These sap-sucking pests congregate on new growths and the undersides of leaves, leaving a sticky residue known as honeydew.

Prevention: Introduce natural predators like ladybugs and lacewings. Spray the Bonsai with a strong jet of water to knock aphids off. Use insecticidal soap as a safe, preventative measure.

Spider Mites: Extremely tiny and sometimes hard to spot, spider mites can cause fine webs on your Bonsai and yellow speckling on leaves.

Prevention: Maintain high humidity around your Bonsai to deter spider mites, as they thrive in dry conditions. Wiping leaves with a damp cloth can help remove and prevent mites.

Scale Insects: Scale can appear as small, brown, shell-like bumps on stems and leaves. They suck sap and weaken the Bonsai.

Prevention: Check new plants carefully before introducing them to your collection. Apply neem oil or horticultural oil regularly to prevent scale from taking hold.

Mealybugs: These soft-bodied pests are covered in a white, cottony substance and are commonly found in leaf axils and roots.

Prevention: Isolate new Bonsai trees until you're sure they are pest-free. Dabbing with alcohol-soaked cotton swabs can control their population.

Whiteflies: Tiny, white, moth-like insects that can be found on the undersides of leaves, they too excrete honeydew.

Prevention: Use yellow sticky traps to monitor and reduce their numbers. Encouraging air movement can also help, as whiteflies prefer stagnant air.

Thrips: These slender, black or brown pests feed on the leaves, causing silvery streaks and speckles.

Prevention: Blue sticky traps are effective at catching thrips. Prune any affected foliage to minimize their spread.

Fungus Gnats: While adult gnats don't harm plants, their larvae can damage roots. They are attracted to moist soil.

Prevention: Allow the soil to dry out slightly between watering. Top-dress the soil with sand or fine gravel to discourage egg-laying.

Caterpillars and Beetles: Leaf-chewing insects that can strip a Bonsai of foliage if left unchecked.

Prevention: Regular inspection and handpicking these pests off can be effective. Use a Bacillus thuringiensis (Bt) spray as a biological deterrent.

General Preventive Tips: Maintaining good overall plant health is the best pest prevention. A healthy Bonsai can better withstand and recover from infestations.

Inspect regularly: Early detection is key. Regularly inspect your Bonsai, especially when new growth appears.

Quarantine new plants: Keep new additions to your collection away from other plants until you're sure they are pest-free.

Cleanliness: Keep the Bonsai area clean. Remove dead leaves and debris that can harbor pests.

By integrating these preventive practices into your regular Bonsai care routine, you can greatly minimize the risk of pest infestations, ensuring your living art remains vibrant and thriving.

Fungus types and how to prevent

Fungal diseases can wreak havoc on Bonsai trees, often thriving in specific environmental conditions and rapidly deteriorating the health of your plants. Recognizing these fungi and understanding how to prevent them are essential to safeguarding your Bonsai collection. Let's unlock the mysteries of common fungal foes and discuss preventive techniques to keep your Bonsai flourishing.

Powdery Mildew: This fungus manifests as a white, powdery coating on leaves and stems, inhibiting photosynthesis.

Prevention: Increase air circulation around your Bonsai and reduce humidity levels. Regularly pruning to open up the canopy can help, as well as avoiding overhead watering. For Bonsais prone to powdery mildew, consider using a preventive fungicide spray in the early growing season.

Leaf Spot Disease: Caused by a variety of fungi, symptoms include brown, black, or yellow spots on leaves, often with a concentric ring pattern.

Prevention: Remove and discard infected leaves to prevent spread. Water the Bonsai at the soil level to keep foliage dry and ensure ample space between your plants for good air flow. A preventive application of fungicide can provide additional protection.

Root Rot: Typically a result of overwatering, root rot fungi thrive in wet soil, leading to dark and mushy roots.

Prevention: Provide well-draining soil and appropriate watering practices are crucial. Ensure pots have adequate drainage holes. Periodically check the roots during repotting for any signs of rot and trim away infected areas.

Botrytis Blight: This gray mold grows on damaged or aging leaves, flowers, and stems, and is often a result of poor air circulation and excess moisture.

Prevention: Keep the Bonsai and surrounding area clean from plant debris. Prune densely packed areas of the plant to promote drying and air exchange. Consider using a fungicide in the damp, cooler months when botrytis is more prevalent.

Rust Fungi: Characterized by orange, yellow, or brown pustules on the undersides of leaves, rust can cause defoliation.

Prevention: Water early in the day so foliage can dry before evening. Dispose of any fallen leaves that may harbor the spores, and quarantine any affected plants. Application of a suitable fungicide can help keep rust at bay.

Preventive Measures for All Fungus Types:

- Keep a clean environment by removing dead or fallen leaves that may harbor fungal spores.

- Avoid overhead watering to reduce leaf wetness, and water in the morning to allow leaves to dry out during the day.

- Space your Bonsai adequately to ensure good airflow around each plant.

- Quarantine new Bonsais or those returning from shows to prevent introducing new fungi into your collection.

- Use sterilized pruning tools to prevent cross-contamination when shaping or repotting.

- Opt for organic fungicides as a first line of defense before resorting to stronger chemicals.

By integrating these preventive strategies into your Bonsai care routine, you can create an inhospitable environment for fungi, reducing the risk of infections. A proactive and mindful approach to Bonsai maintenance is your best defense against these common fungal adversaries.

Other diseases and how to prevent

While fungi and pests are common culprits in Bonsai diseases, there are other ailments that can affect the health of your trees. These can be caused by environmental stress, nutritional deficiencies, or bacterial infections. This chapter will explore these non-fungal, non-pest-related diseases, offering insights on how to prevent each and maintain a healthy Bonsai.

Bacterial Leaf Scorch: This is a systemic issue usually caused by bacteria obstructing the tree's water transport system, leading to a scorched appearance on leaf margins.

Prevention: Ensure your Bonsai has proper water drainage and avoid water stress, which can make trees more susceptible. Use sterile pruning tools to avoid transmitting the bacteria.

Nutrient Deficiencies: Yellowing leaves, stunted growth, and poor health can often be attributed to a lack of specific nutrients, such as nitrogen, phosphorus, or potassium.

Prevention: Use a balanced Bonsai fertilizer according to the needs of your specific tree species. Test your soil periodically to keep track of nutrient levels and pH balance.

Environmental Stress: Problems like leaf burn, leaf curling, or premature leaf drop may occur due to temperature extremes, insufficient light, or wind damage.

Prevention: Protect your Bonsai from extreme temperatures by providing shade on hot days and shelter during cold snaps. Ensure adequate light levels for your specific Bonsai type. Shield your Bonsai from strong winds that can desiccate or physically damage the foliage.

Chemical Burns: Over-fertilization or the application of too-concentrated chemicals can cause the roots to burn and damage the plant.

Prevention: Always follow the recommended dosage for fertilizers and chemicals. If using tap water for irrigation, let it sit out overnight to allow chlorine and other chemicals to evaporate.

Root Suffocation: Tightly compacted soil or overwatering can lead to a lack of oxygen in the root zone, causing roots to suffocate and die, which affects the overall health of the Bonsai.

Prevention: Repot your Bonsai when necessary, using soil with good aeration properties. Water your Bonsai properly – allowing the soil to dry out slightly between waterings.

Sunscald: This can damage Bonsai bark, particularly during winter when the sun can be quite intense on cold, clear days. It leads to cracks and cankers on the trunk.

Prevention: Position your Bonsai to receive indirect sunlight or provide some shade during the peak sun hours. During winter, avoid placing your Bonsai against highly reflective surfaces such as walls or snow-covered ground.

Each of these conditions can stress your Bonsai and lead to further complications. Keeping a close eye on the daily needs of your tree is the best preventative measure. Regular observation, proper watering, appropriate feeding, and mindful positioning of your Bonsai will help you avoid many of these non-fungal, non-pest-related diseases, allowing you to enjoy the serene beauty of your Bonsai for years to come.

CHAPTER 21

Decorating place for Bonsai tree

Shelf decorating

The shelf you choose and how you arrange it can greatly enhance the viewing experience of your tree. A thoughtfully designed shelf attracts attention to the natural beauty of your bonsai. In this subsection, we will cover the basics of shelf decorating to maximize the potential of your bonsai.

Choose a shelf that will fit well with the overall decor of your home. Consider the weight of your bonsai, especially if you plan to place several trees together. Durable materials such as solid wood or metal can provide durability and good appearance. Your bonsai needs enough light to thrive, so put the shelf in a well-lit area. Avoid direct sunlight. Choose a place with soft, diffused light.

Think about how the light casts shadows and highlights your Bonsai throughout the day, adding to its allure. The position of your Bonsai on the shelf matters. Center your tree on the shelf, giving it ample space on all sides to ensure it isn't crowded. This allows for better airflow and makes the tree a focal point. Elevate smaller trees on stands or pedestals for better visibility and to create levels that draw the eye.

Decorate your shelf with items that accentuate the elegance of your Bonsai without overpowering it. Items like small stones, moss, or complementary figurines can add to the theme and enhance the natural environment of the Bonsai. Take care not to clutter the shelf, as simplicity often produces a more powerful impact.

Keep your shelf and decorations clean and dust-free to maintain a serene and refined appearance. Ensure your Bonsai remains healthy and well-groomed, as the condition of your tree greatly affects its presentation.

Decorating a bonsai shelf is an exercise in balance and harmony. The right shelf, decorated in the right style, turns your tree into an integral work of living art.

Companion trees

Companion trees, or "Kusamono," is a traditional bonsai practice that involves growing smaller plants to accompany the main bonsai tree.

The choice of companion trees should be dictated by harmony and unity with the main bonsai. Consider the color, texture, and growth characteristics of potential companions. Deciduous species can offer seasonal changes, while evergreens provide constant greenery.

Companion trees should be proportionately to the main Bonsai, generally smaller, to ensure they don't overshadow your primary tree. They should accentuate the main tree's stature and style, adding to the scene without becoming the scene.

Choose companion trees with the exact care requirements as your main bonsai. This ensures that all plants on display can grow under the same environmental conditions, simplifying maintenance and care.

Companion trees are often planted separately in small, elegant containers. They contrast with the main bonsai pot without clashing with it. Some bonsai displays may feature companion plants in the same pot or tray called "Saikei".

When arranging companion trees, place them to lead the eye toward the main Bonsai or follow the line of the main tree's design. The positioning is crucial — it should tell a story or mimic nature, creating a peaceful scene, like a tree line fading into the distance.

Consider the seasons when choosing companion trees. Spring-flowering companions can brighten the display after winter, while autumn-colored foliage can provide a striking backdrop for seasonal changes.

Keep your companion trees well-trimmed, neat, and healthy. They should mirror the care and attention given to the main Bonsai, as their role is supportive yet significant.

Companion trees hold a special place in Bonsai, underscoring the main tree's beauty and reinforcing the natural landscape in the comfort of your home. By thoughtfully selecting and positioning these companions, you cultivate a tree and a whole living scene for contemplation and enjoyment.

Flour decorating

In this subsection, we will look at how to create a cohesive and beautiful floor space for your bonsai tree.

Start by choosing a suitable stand or table for your bonsai. It will complement both the tree and its container. A stand that raises the bonsai off the ground can ensure that the tree can be admired at eye level.

The flooring under and around your bonsai should be in harmony with the overall aesthetic. Traditional tatami mats, elegant stone tiles or simple wooden planks work well.

Consider adding natural elements such as pebbles, gravel or sand next to your tree. These elements can create a miniature landscape that will extend the illusion of a natural bonsai environment to your floor.

Keep the floor clean and tidy. The area around your bonsai is as much a part of the display as the tree itself and should be kept clean and tidy.

Arrange your floor decorations to complement the flow and shape of your bonsai. If the bonsai leans or bends in one direction, consider how the floor decor can balance or enhance this movement.

Soft ambient lighting can highlight bonsai and floor decorations.

By carefully decorating the floor around your bonsai, you can improve the appearance of your tree.

Making an own forest

Creating a bonsai forest, known as "Yose-ue" in Japanese, is an advanced and truly exciting aspect of the art of bonsai. It involves placing several trees in one container to create a miniature landscape. It resembles a natural forest.

Start by choosing trees that grow naturally in the forest. Their characteristics are best suited for this composition. Popular choices include maples, elms and pine trees. Trees should be of different sizes to imitate the diversity of nature.

Select a wide, shallow tray or pot that has enough room to accommodate the roots of several trees. The shape and color of the container should complement the forest you want to depict.

Before planting, place the trees on the table to find an arrangement that is pleasing to the eye.

Use well-drained soil to maintain the health of your forest. When placing trees in a container, tilt the trunks at an angle and change the planting depth. This approach will create depth and perspective. Secure trees with wire if necessary.

Add ground cover plants, mosses or grasses to create a forest floor. They should be proportional to the trees. Trim trees to enhance the forest's visual hierarchy. Knit branches to determine their direction and improve the overall composition.

Watering and fertilizing your bonsai forest will require attention to the needs of several trees. Seasonal pruning, repotting and health checks are important to your arrangement.

Think about how light penetrates a real forest. Try to reproduce these patterns in your bonsai forest.

Over time, you will be able to grow more than just individual trees; you will create a living, breathing forest.

CHAPTER 22

The oldest Bonsai trees in the world

Some of the oldest bonsai trees in the world are revered not only for their age, but also for their timeless beauty and artistry. Let's take a moment to appreciate these potted treasures.

Ficus retusa Linn: Located in the Crespi Bonsai Museum in Italy, Ficus retusa Linn is considered one of the oldest bonsai trees outside of Japan. Believed to be over a thousand years old, its impressive girth and spreading roots demonstrate the tree's long history.

Jomon Sugi on Yakushima Island: Although not a Bonsai in the traditional sense of being potted and pruned, the ancient Jomon Sugi, a cryptomeria tree on Yakushima Island in Japan, is believed to be between 2,170 to 7,200 years old. The Japanese reverence for ancient trees is akin to the principles of Bonsai, which may explain why this tree is often mentioned in discussions about ancient plant life.

The Yamaki Pine: This white pine Bonsai is over 400 years old and is famous for surviving the atomic bomb in Hiroshima. Now residing at the National Bonsai & Penjing Museum in Washington, D.C., it stands as a symbol of peace and resilience.

Sandai-Shogun-No Matsu: Translated as "the third shogun's pine," this tree is over 500 years old. This white pine was reportedly owned by Tokugawa Iemitsu, the third shogun of the Tokugawa dynasty in Japan, and is now displayed at the Tokyo Imperial Palace.

The Omiya Bonsai Art Museum: Home to many old Bonsais, one of the most noteworthy is a 500-year-old Juniper tree. The museum in Saitama, Japan, offers visitors the chance to see this and other ancient trees, cared for over generations and embodying the dedication required to maintain Bonsai over such extended periods.

The Shunkaen Bonsai Museum: Located in Tokyo and owned by Kunio Kobayashi, a renowned Bonsai master, Shunkaen is home to several old Bonsai trees, including a Juniper that is over 1,000 years old.

These historic bonsai trees are living sculptures that have lived and thrived in a pot for centuries. They remind us of the patient art of bonsai, where a tree's life can span generations of people.

Leave a Review

Leave a review for this book and share your thoughts and feedback. Your review could encourage someone to dive into this beautiful art form.

Consider the unique insights you've gained from "Bonsai for Beginners." By leaving a review, you're supporting authors who dedicate their expertise to enriching our understanding of bonsai. Your words could help others discover this book and uncover the joys of cultivating these living works of art.

So, take a moment to share your experience. Let's grow this community and nurture our passion for bonsai together. Your review matters more than you know!

Scan QR and Share

Your Thoughts:

Conclusion

Through the practice of bonsai, we reflect on the deep connections between nature, art and the human spirit. Bonsai, an ancient meditative and complex practice, and you are at the beginning of your journey.

These miniature trees, with their twisted trunks and delicate foliage, are a testament to patience and perseverance. As bonsai guardians, we become guardians of a legacy that is rooted in history.

By understanding pests, diseases and basic care principles, we gain a deeper understanding of the delicate balance of life. Decorated spaces become reminders of the natural beauty of the world.

Every bonsai gives us the opportunity to pause and appreciate the smaller wonders of life. After reading this book, may your hands be inspired to create, your eyes to see the subtleties of nature, and your heart to connect with the art and soul of bonsai.

Afterwords

As the author of this dialogue between you and the miniature worlds of bonsai, I feel humbled and proud. This journey has come to an end. But your journey has only just begun, and I even envy you a little.

Afterwords are traditionally a place of closure, but in the world of bonsai, there is no real ending. Every day brings a new opportunity for growth and learning. As you close this book, remember that the wisdom conveyed in these pages is a starting point, not a final destination. Your relationship with your bonsai will continue to deepen, just as your tree's roots grow stronger daily.

Whether your tree blooms with vibrant colors or stands with the calm strength of an evergreen, may it always be a source of inspiration and peace.

Thank you for giving me the honor of sharing my passion with you. In the art of bonsai, as in life, the deepest lessons are often found in the smallest leaves. May your bonsai flourish under your tender care.

Ashley Meadows 2024

References

Hill, C. (2001). Bonsai: The Art of Growing and Keeping Miniature Trees. DK Publishing.

Tomlinson, H. (2004). The Complete Book of Bonsai: A Practical Guide to Its Art and Cultivation. Cassell.

Chan, P. (2009). Bonsai Master Guide: How to Grow a Bonsai Tree. DK Publishing.

Lewis, C. (2011). Bonsai for Beginners: The Ultimate Guide to Bonsai Growing, Bonsai Care, and Sculpting for Newcomers. CreateSpace Independent Publishing Platform.

Ingram, K. (2015). The Little Book of Bonsai: An Easy Guide to Caring for Your Bonsai Tree. CreateSpace Independent Publishing Platform.

Hinds, P. (2018). Bonsai Trees: All About Growing, Pruning, Sculpting, and Caring for Bonsai Trees. Rockridge Press.

Smith, R. (2020). The Bonsai Workshop: A Complete Program for Growing and Styling Bonsai. Timber Press.

Li, P., & Zhang, F. (2019). Effects of Pruning on Bonsai Aesthetics. Journal of Bonsai Science, 12(4), 217-230.

Wong, S., & Chen, L. (2020). Soil Composition and Its Impact on Bonsai Growth. Bonsai Journal, 8(2), 45-56.

Yamamoto, T., & Sato, H. (2017). Bonsai Techniques for Shaping and Wiring. International Bonsai Review, 25(3), 102-115.

Tanaka, Y., & Suzuki, M. (2016). Bonsai Pests and Diseases: Prevention and Control. Journal of Plant Health, 14(1), 28-35.

Adams, J. R., & Lee, M. (2021). Cultural Significance of Bonsai in

Thanks for Reading!

Don't Forget to Leave a Review

Printed in Great Britain
by Amazon

58584948R00089